ACT for Neurological Conditions

ACT FOR NEUROLOGICAL CONDITIONS

Acceptance and Commitment Therapy
for People with Acquired Brain Injury
and Progressive Neurological Conditions

Edited by Kim Fletcher and Amanda Mobley

Illustrations by Masha Pimas

Jessica Kingsley Publishers
London and Philadelphia

First published in Great Britain in 2026 by Jessica Kingsley Publishers
An imprint of John Murray Press

2

Copyright © Kim Fletcher and Amanda Mobley 2026

The right of Kim Fletcher and Amanda Mobley to be identified as
the Author of the Work has been asserted by them in accordance
with the Copyright, Designs and Patents Act 1988.

Chapter 2 © Kristy Potter, Rebecca Cramp and Amanda Mobley, Chapter 3 © Maria
Dale, Lee Bell-Jones and Katie Melvin, Chapter 4 © Lorraine King, Natalie Hampson and
Emily Bunn, Chapter 5 © James Briggs, Chapter 6 © Dana Wong and Nick Sathananthan,
Chapter 7 © Rebecca Gould, Chapter 8 © Nima Golijani-Moghaddam and Anna Tickle

A CIP catalogue record for this title is available from the
British Library and the Library of Congress

ISBN 978 1 78775 792 9
eISBN 978 1 78775 793 6

Printed and bound in the United States by Integrated Books International

Jessica Kingsley Publishers' policy is to use papers that are natural, renewable
and recyclable products and made from wood grown in sustainable
forests. The logging and manufacturing processes are expected to conform
to the environmental regulations of the country of origin.

Jessica Kingsley Publishers
Carmelite House
50 Victoria Embankment
London EC4Y 0DZ

www.jkp.com

John Murray Press
Part of Hodder & Stoughton Ltd
An Hachette Company

The authorised representative in the EEA is Hachette Ireland,
8 Castlecourt Centre, Dublin 15, D15 XTP3, Ireland (email: info@hbgi.ie)

Contents

CHAPTER 1

Introduction

'It's all wrong. By rights we shouldn't even be here. But we are. It's like in the great stories... The ones that really mattered. Full of darkness and danger they were, and sometimes you didn't want to know the end. Because how could the end be happy. How could the world go back to the way it was when so much bad happened. But in the end, it's only a passing thing, this shadow. Even darkness must pass. A new day will come. And when the sun shines it will shine out the clearer. Those were the stories that stayed with you. That meant something.'
SAM'S SPEECH, *LORD OF THE RINGS: THE TWO TOWERS* (JACKSON, 2002)

Navigating life with a neurological condition can present unique challenges, sudden changes in life circumstances, unpredictable future events and loss of control. Negotiating the waves of these experiences requires flexibility and willingness to let go of control of the tide.

When diagnosed or living with a neurological condition, people often describe the state of being between two stages, or on the precipice of transitioning to something new and unknown. Disorientation and ambiguity can drive behaviour, and waves come in thick and fast, with people often wanting to turn away or hide from complex emotional experiences. The development of clear formulations encompassing thoughts, feelings, actions and sociocultural context is a starting point for all coherent psychological intervention, and acceptance and commitment therapy (ACT) is no different. Understanding the interaction between, for example, changes in cognitive ability and emotional distress as well as consequent actions is fundamental to developing effective interventions.

This book is structured around the ACT hexaflex, which highlights the key principles and cornerstones of this approach. The hexaflex includes sections on opening up to experiences (willingness, cognitive defusion), bringing awareness to the present moment (present moment awareness, self-as-context) and living the life you want to live (committed action, values). The hexaflex does not have a start and end point and is designed to be used flexibly within sessions, responding to what the person has brought and current experiential knowledge. As such, this book is not designed to be followed in a linear fashion either, but the areas of the hexaflex can be used according to need.

This book also uses the term 'neurological condition' or people with neurological conditions (pwNCs) in a broad sense to encompass those with both acquired conditions such as traumatic brain injury and stroke as well as those with progressive conditions such as Huntington's disease. In this book we have brought together clinicians working in different healthcare contexts, to help understand how ACT can be applied and adapted. Traditional psychological therapy, such as cognitive behaviour therapy (CBT), offers avenues for support focused on changing the content and nature of the thoughts and finding alternative rational and logical ways to respond. Third-wave behavioural approaches, such as ACT, build on this by considering our relationship with thoughts and how this impacts day-to-day life.

We encourage you to immerse yourself in this book. Hold this text lightly and take from it what is helpful alongside your own knowledge, experience and other excellent work and resources available. Allow yourself to lean into flexibility in practice, feel inspired, learn something new and dive deeper into those areas that capture your interest, imagination and creativity.

Reference

Jackson, P. (Director). (2002). *Lord of the Rings: The Two Towers* [Film]. WingNut Films. New Line Cinema.

CHAPTER 2

Willingness

KRISTY POTTER, REBECCA CRAMP AND AMANDA MOBLEY

About the authors

Kristy Potter is a clinical psychologist who is currently working in general practice in Guernsey, and was previously in Bermuda. Before this, she worked with Rebecca Cramp (senior assistant psychologist) in the Defence Medical Rehabilitation Centre (DMRC) in the neuro-rehabilitation team for the Ministry of Defence. During this period of working together, they embedded ACT in their practice, both within the individual work they were undertaking as well as in the system and organisation. This experience has allowed them to develop the use of ACT with people with neurological conditions, in particular in the design of specific adaptations.

Prior to working at DMRC, Kristy spent time working with older adults and people with intellectual disabilities, and within an inpatient setting. She also has a background in research, having published reviews of cognitive rehabilitation as well as original research studies, for example using an ACT telephone-supported bibliotherapy for carers of people with multiple sclerosis.

Rebecca Cramp currently works at DMRC and has also worked with looked-after children and in a community neurological rehabilitation team. She has an undergraduate degree in psychology with cognitive neuroscience and a master's in rehabilitation psychology.

Amanda Mobley currently works as a consultant clinical neuropsychologist with adults and children who have acquired and progressive neurological conditions.

What is willingness?

When we talk about 'willingness' in ACT, we are referring to the umbrella concept around 'acceptance'. However, the term acceptance can raise complex responses in the context of neurological conditions, so we have used 'willingness' in place of 'acceptance' within this chapter. 'Willingness' is the ability to be open to thoughts, feelings, images, bodily sensations or any other experience, whether internal or external.

The cognitively inflexible counterpart to willingness is 'unwillingness' and 'avoidance', whereby someone is unwilling (consciously or unconsciously) to have the experiences associated with the brain injury or neurological condition and will avoid these. This also includes 'experiential avoidance' where a person is unwilling to have the internal feeling associated with this experience (for an expanded discussion on experienced denial, please see Chapter 5 on self-as-context). However, avoidance, both physical and experiential, comes at a cost. This cost might be loss of previously enjoyed and valued activities, fatigue associated with trying to avoid internal experiences or loss of emotional range and numbness. For example, someone with expressive aphasia following a stroke may feel uncomfortable, embarrassed or upset when speaking to others. This may then lead them to avoid other people in an attempt to prevent feelings of sadness or embarrassment, leading to a restricted social circle and them spending more time alone and becoming isolated. By avoiding uncomfortable emotions, this individual is not only restricting their world, but also potentially reducing opportunities for ongoing rehabilitation.

Furthermore, experiential avoidance and unwillingness to have a particular thought or emotion actually increases the chance of having that thought or experience. For example, if you have the thought 'don't think about chocolate cake', you inevitably think about chocolate cake. In order to remind yourself not to think about it, you have to remember what it is you are trying to avoid.

Key principles

What often shows up for people when we talk about acceptance or willingness is this idea that we are expecting them to 'like' or 'want' the painful feeling or experience. This is not necessarily the case. When we refer to willingness or acceptance, we are looking to find a way to sit with painful thoughts, feelings, emotions or experiences in service of something that is important to our clients, tapping into their values and driving factors.

The other side of 'willingness' is of equal, if not greater, importance; this is the idea of being open *without struggle*. We often try to struggle against certain emotions and label and name them as fundamentally 'bad' or 'negative'. Part of this is more systemic – society's way of telling us that we 'shouldn't' feel this pain, fear or discomfort – and the other part of this is the internal argument we have within ourselves regarding these uncomfortable thoughts and feelings due to classifying them as 'problems' or 'negative' emotions.

The key principles of the work in this part of the hexaflex involves bringing awareness to experiential avoidance and considering the costs that this avoidance has on living a life in accordance with their values, also known as 'workability'.

Importance of willingness for people with neurological conditions

When we consider something as life-altering or assumption-shattering, such as receiving a diagnosis of a degenerative neurological condition, or having a sudden onset acquired brain injury, there is often an understandable natural instinct to push away or avoid the emotional pain associated with this experience. However, as the diagnosis cannot be avoided itself, this can often lead to avoidance or lack of engagement with meaningful and valued activity. Willingness is thereby important to allow people with neurological conditions to be open to the discomfort and pain that show up when they think about the diagnosis and about loss or areas of adaptation, in order to continue to live a full and valued life and gain psychological flexibility. Willingness in this context encourages openness to experiencing these painful emotions and predictions for their future. We do not expect, or even hope for, clients to 'want' to 'like' this, but instead encourage them to be open to noticing and acknowledging what shows up in order to work towards a full and valued life, tapping into values-based goal setting and psychological flexibility as a whole.

As with all ACT processes, it is often much easier to consider concepts through use of metaphors. One such metaphor to describe willingness is to consider that the painful thought, feeling, experience you are avoiding or struggling against is much like holding something spikey, perhaps a thorned rose, in your hands. If you were to really hold on to this firmly, it's going to prick you, it's going to dig in; effectively it's going to cause you pain and discomfort. Willingness is like holding it gently, holding it close to you, so that it no longer impacts you in the same way, and you can now go about your day holding this painful experience close but without it digging in.

When we consider this in the context of neurological conditions, we encourage people to be willing to experience things in a new and more flexible way. Therefore, we believe that ACT with clients in neurological rehabilitation is flexible and accessible both in structured individual therapy as well as in indirect work, through interdisciplinary teams. This might take the form of supporting the client's willingness to be open to the use of strategies, supporting colleagues to break down barriers to engagement or more structured individual therapy. As well as client flexibility, it's important to consider ourselves flexible as therapists. It is particularly key for us as therapists to consider our own willingness to sit with the difficult emotions, thoughts and even judgements that we might notice in ourselves. Ultimately, we can also use this concept to notice, name and be willing to sit with uncomfortable emotions within a staff team, as well as on an individual level.

Evidence for the use of willingness

There is a dearth of literature regarding willingness as a specific process within the process-based ACT literature. ACT, in its relative infancy, has not yet received the same level of funding as more traditional psychotherapies. However, more recently, we have seen the inclusion of ACT within the UK National Institute for Health and Care Excellence guidelines for pain (NICE, 2021); helpfully there are areas of generalisations here which can be applied within neurological conditions.

Similarly to working with people with neurological conditions, ACT-based pain interventions see willingness and acceptance as central to the mechanism of change. These are used primarily as a tool to foster openness to experience, allowing people to adapt their lives in light of their chronic pain experiences (in a value-driven manner); this in turn has been shown to lead to better emotional outcomes. For example, Fish *et al.* (2013) highlighted that acceptance and willingness of pain mediated the relationship with pain severity and emotional distress, and those with increased acceptance of their pain had better outcomes with measures of depression, anxiety, pain interference, catastrophising, increased psychological flexibility and higher satisfaction with life. Similar results to this have been noted in other presentations (e.g. OCD: Reid *et al.*, 2017; workplace stress: Bond & Bunce, 2000).

When we consider the ACT literature for people with neurological conditions, willingness also appears to be a key mechanism of change. For example, a recent study highlighting the use of ACT as effective for reducing psychological distress in a traumatic brain injury population (Sander *et al.*, 2021) showed effective reduction in symptomatology measures as well as ACT process measures. This highlighted a need for adaptation for cognitive deficits and flexibility in approach. Indeed, given the central aspect of the hexaflex being around psychological flexibility, it must be acknowledged that for some individuals with neurological conditions, particularly those struggling with impact on executive functioning, there is the potential for difficulties in adopting a more psychologically flexible approach to their experiences due to a primary cognitive deficit. Whiting *et al.* (2017) explored this in more detail, considering how the concepts of cognitive and psychological flexibility overlap. Overall, psychological flexibility seems a more overarching construct and cognitive flexibility a sub-component. Therefore, if an individual has difficulties in cognitive flexibility/rigidity as a result of a neurological condition, it may be important to hold in mind this overlap with cognitive and psychological flexibility and be holistic in consideration of avoidance in line with difficulties with executive functioning as well as psychological factors.

Adaptations within the context of neurological conditions

Clients with neurological conditions come with a wide range of socio-cultural heritage and narratives. Therefore, it is important to consider the client's specific needs, and tailor your use of ACT-based interventions accordingly. Some key areas of adaptations focus primarily on adapting communication to the client, considering cognitive profile as well as pre-morbid narratives on thoughts, feelings and emotions. Metaphors and analogies are such a key part of ACT and are designed to make abstract concepts more concrete in nature. It can be helpful to adapt the metaphors to your client's specific difficulties and their specific hobbies and areas of interest.

ACT is already well versed in using videos as a means for communicating complex information. These can be a great resource and facilitate the opportunity to pause and allow additional time for processing and unpicking of the metaphors. People with neurological conditions may have a greater need for breaking down the analogies and unpicking these more formally, often with the use of pictures and drawing. This can be a powerful technique as it can help to give a new language when talking about thoughts and feelings, and allows clients who may have communication difficulties to use metaphors or visual representations to describe their emotions and experiences, for example 'it's cloudy, it's stormy', alongside more traditional emotion language.

Assessment of willingness

There are a number of more formal and informal ways to measure willingness. Informal assessment of this can include noticing and naming the avoidance, and using this to continually drip feed the concepts of willingness to the client. The main process-based measures of ACT also include aspects of willingness, for example the

Comprehensive Assessment of Acceptance and Commitment Therapy (CompACT) (Francis, Dawson & Golijani-Moghaddam, 2016) and the Acceptance and Action Questionnaire-II (AAQ-II) (Bond *et al.*, 2011). The CompACT questionnaire helpfully includes openness to experience as a distinct subsection, which can aid in assessing someone's baseline of openness. However, as a mechanism of change, there is debate in the literature regarding the use of process-based measures. The overall aim of ACT is not to reduce symptoms but instead work towards a rich and meaningful life. Therefore, all assessment should hold this in mind and move away from a focus on symptom reduction.

Introducing willingness to our clients

Introducing the concept of willingness is a multi-layered process which builds on the work on 'being present' and noticing what shows up and the judgements that come up alongside. Initial discussion about willingness may focus on brief exercises to highlight the role of experiential avoidance, such as 'don't think about chocolate cake'.

This leads on to noticing experiential avoidance in their own life, for example thoughts or feelings which they may be avoiding. Exploration can then extend to 'workability' and engaging clients in discussion around what they have tried to help them avoid the painful experiences associated with the neurological condition, what has worked and what it has cost. Ultimately, the aim is to establish that control strategies do not, and will not, work in the long term and to foster an openness to explore alternatives to control.

Useful metaphors and experiential exercises for developing willingness

Clients with neurological conditions can report feeling that 'if I accept it, that means I am giving up'. Especially within a neurological rehabilitation setting, there is frequently a view of 'more in – more out' and the harder people work on their rehabilitation the better the outcomes for them. However, for the majority of people with neurological conditions, it is not a simple linear relationship and there are multiple factors that have to be balanced in order to make meaningful progress. It is not the case that if they just work harder they will be able to leave the brain injury behind.

This means that often when we work with clients on willingness within a neurological setting, we may need initially to work on developing this notion of 'progress' and drawing on models such as the Y-shaped model (Gracey, Evans & Malley, 2009), which highlights that rehabilitation is the coming together of the past and the present self to forge a new path incorporating both aspects of experience. We try to foster willingness and openness to this 'new' self rather than focus on returning to the 'previous' self.

Here are some examples of useful metaphors and approaches to this work for people with neurological conditions:

- *Quicksand* (Hayes, Pankey & Gregg, 2002): If you get stuck in quicksand, the first instinct is to struggle and try to get free. However, the more you struggle, the more stuck you become and the deeper you sink. For example, it is common to see people trying to manage neurological fatigue initially by trying to 'fight through', ending up in a boom-and-bust cycle. The alternative approach to managing quicksand may be counterintuitive – to not struggle, to lie flat and expand your contact with the surface of the sand. Similarly, the alternative approach to managing fatigue is not to struggle, to recognise when fatigue is present and spread out your energy levels.

- *Drop the rope* (Harris, 2009): Imagine you are in a tug of war with a monster, with you at one end of the rope and a monster such as a brain injury at the other end, and a bottomless pit between you. The monster keeps pulling you towards the pit and you are putting more and more effort into trying to pull away. The control strategies are different ways of still pulling on the rope but there are other options, for example you can drop the rope. That doesn't change that the monster is still there, but you are not involved in struggling or fighting it.

- *Unwanted party guest* (Oliver, 2011): Imagine that the brain injury or neurological condition has come to a party you are giving. You can fight with the guest or kick him out and guard the door, so he doesn't come back in. However, as you are doing that you are not able to enjoy your party. Is there another way to manage this situation whereby you can tolerate the unwelcome guest being there and can continue to enjoy the party?

- *Struggle switch* (Harris, 2022): When painful emotions or thoughts show up, you can have your struggle switch 'on' or 'off'. 'On' means that you fight the feeling or emotion, try to control it, get rid of it, escape from it. However, the outcome of this means that your feelings can escalate, including anger that your strategies are not working or sadness that you are not good enough or able to try hard enough. If the switch is 'off' then the anxiety is still there but it is free from your attempts to control it and so the secondary feelings do not escalate. In people with neurological conditions the struggle switch is often 'on' because of narratives about 'more in – more out' or inadvertent messages throughout rehabilitation encouraging people to 'think positively'. When a painful thought or feeling about the experience of living with a neurological condition shows up, people are predisposed to struggle against this.

- *Willingness to resist an itch:* When you feel itchy you have an impulse to scratch. Scratching works by temporarily blocking the mind with mild pain. However, scratching also has the potential to create wounds and can lead to an itch-scratch cycle where more scratching leads to more itching. What happens if you are willing to notice the urge to itch without scratching? Where do you feel that urge to itch? Where does that urge start and stop? Does it feel constant or does the sensation rise and fall? What is it about that urge that you cannot tolerate?

CASE EXAMPLE – GURJIT

Following a stroke, while in inpatient rehabilitation, Gurjit experienced intense bursts of emotional lability where he would spontaneously, and often suddenly, burst into tears at minor triggers, such as being asked how he or his family were and seeing adverts on the television. This was a significant change for Gurjit, and he found this created high levels of shame and self-criticism. This high level of emotion then tended to escalate the episodes. As a result, he was highly anxious when family came to visit, which typically made the labile episodes more likely, and so he refused to see them. As the labile episodes were sudden and frequently loud, ward staff would tend to respond with multiple staff members attending, trying to calm Gurjit down. However, this increased attention and focus resulted in increased attempts to control and often further escalation in the emotion.

Initially, sessions focused on discussions around what he had tried, considering control strategies for the labile episodes and whether these had worked effectively or not. Sessions were also held with the staff to explore the same – what had been tried and whether this had worked. This developed into awareness for Gurjit, his family and the care team that current ways of trying to control the labile episodes were not working. The quicksand metaphor was used to support understanding that struggling against the lability was making him more stuck. Alternatives were explored, such as the struggle switch, enabling him and the staff team to experience the labile episode without struggle.

References

Bond, F. W. & Bunce, D. (2000). Mediators of change in emotion-focused and problem-focused worksite stress management interventions. *Journal of Occupational Health Psychology*, 5, 156.

Bond, F. W., Hayes, S. C., Baer, R. A., Carpenter, K. M. *et al.* (2011). Preliminary psychometric properties of the Acceptance and Action Questionnaire – II: A revised measure of psychological inflexibility and experiential avoidance. *Behavior Therapy*, 42, 676–688.

Fish, R. A., Hogan, M. J., Morrison, T. G., Stewart, I. & McGuire, B. E. (2013). Willing and able: A closer look at pain willingness and activity engagement on the Chronic Pain Acceptance Questionnaire (CPAQ-8). *The Journal of Pain*, 14(3), 233–245.

Francis, A. W., Dawson, D. L. & Golijani-Moghaddam, N. (2016). The development and validation of the Comprehensive assessment of Acceptance and Commitment Therapy processes (CompACT). *Journal of Contextual Behavioral Science*, 5(3), 134–145.

Gracey, F., Evans, J. & Malley, D. (2009). Capturing process and outcome in complex rehabilitation interventions: A 'Y-shaped' model. *Neuropsychological Rehabilitation*, 19(6), 867–890.

Harris, R. (2009). *ACT Made Simple: An Easy-to-Read Primer on Acceptance and Commitment Therapy*. Oakland, CA: New Harbinger.

Harris, R. (2022). *The Happiness Trap Second Edition: Stop Struggling, Start Living*. London: Little Brown Book Group.

Hayes, S. C., Pankey, J. & Gregg, J. (2002). Chapter 5: Acceptance and Commitment Therapy. In R. A. DiTomasso & E. A. Gosch (eds), *Anxiety Disorders: A Practitioner's Guide to Comparative Treatments*. New York, NY: Springer Publishing Company.

NICE. (2021). Chronic pain (primary & secondary) in over 16s: Assessment of all chronic pain and management of chronic primary pain [NG193]. www.nice.org.uk/guidance/ng193

Oliver, J. (2011). *The Unwelcome Party Guest*. www.youtube.com/watch?v=VYht-guymF4

Reid, A. M., Garner, L. E., Van Kirk, N., Gironda, C. *et al.* (2017). How willing are you? Willingness as a predictor of change during treatment of adults with obsessive-compulsive disorder. *Depression and Anxiety*, 34(11), 1057–1064.

Sander, A. M., Clark, A. N., Arciniegas, D. B., Tran, K. *et al.* (2021). A randomized controlled trial of acceptance and commitment therapy for psychological distress among persons with traumatic brain injury. *Neuropsychological Rehabilitation*, 31(7), 1105–1129.

Whiting, D. L., Deane, F. P., Simpson, G. K., McLeod, H. J. & Ciarrochi, J. (2017). Cognitive and psychological flexibility after a traumatic brain injury and the implications for treatment in acceptance-based therapies: A conceptual review. *Neuropsychological Rehabilitation*, 27(2), 263–299.

CHAPTER 3

Cognitive Defusion

MARIA DALE, LEE BELL-JONES AND KATIE MELVIN

About the authors

Maria Dale is a clinical psychologist who works in a UK specialist Huntington's disease (HD) service for Leicestershire Partnership NHS Trust neuropsychology department. She completed her clinical psychology doctorate at the University of Leicester in 2002 and clinical neuropsychology training at the University of Nottingham in 2011. Maria has published widely in eminent journals for neurology and is currently leading a funded feasibility randomised controlled trial that uses ACT principles with persons with HD (GUIDE-HD) (Dale *et al.*, 2023).

Lee Bell-Jones is an assistant psychologist who also works in a specialist HD service, based within the clinical neuropsychology department for Leicestershire Partnership NHS Trust. He completed his master's in psychology at Coventry University in 2020. Lee has assisted in the development and implementation of ACT-based materials for the GUIDE-HD project and is undertaking a service evaluation of mindfulness sessions for individuals with HD.

Katie Melvin is a clinical psychologist working in neuropsychology for Leicestershire Partnership NHS Trust's HD service and Noah's Ark Children's Hospital for Wales. Katie completed her doctorate in clinical psychology at the University of Leicester in 2022, after completing her PhD at the University of Leicester in 2020, and psychological wellbeing practitioner training with the University of Exeter in 2016. Alongside using ACT clinically, Katie collaborates in developing, delivering and supervising the GUIDE-HD trial.

Introduction

This chapter will outline cognitive fusion and defusion. We will examine why people with neurological conditions (pwNCs) may benefit from exercises that promote cognitive defusion and discuss how 'cognitive defusion exercises' can be adapted to meet the needs of pwNCs. We will briefly examine what work on cognitive defusion has been undertaken among this group. Further to this, we will discuss how methods that promote cognitive defusion can be used for pwNCs and provide a fictional case example. Finally, we will provide worksheets that can be used in clinical practice.

What is cognitive fusion and cognitive defusion?

Cognitive *fusion* refers to the times when we struggle to separate ourselves from our thoughts. In a state of cognitive fusion, we can become so entangled with our thoughts and other internal processes, such as beliefs and memories, that we tend to see these as representing reality. Hence, when we are cognitively fused, we may find it difficult to engage with the world outside our own heads and can become rigid in our thinking.

In a state of cognitive *defusion*, we can notice thoughts as simply thoughts without getting caught up in them and can choose to respond to them flexibly. This can involve simply watching our thoughts, accepting them and letting go of them if we choose to. In other words, we become an observer of our thoughts. Several authors have identified that the term 'cognitive defusion' is used interchangeably to describe a procedure, process and outcome (Assaz *et al.*, 2018, 2022; De Houwer, Barnes-Holmes & Barnes-Holmes, 2016; McEnteggart *et al.*, 2015) and that more precise definitions should be used. Assaz and colleagues recently argued that for the greater pragmatic utility of the term, cognitive defusion should be used to describe an outcome (i.e. a state that a person finds themselves in if they are able to separate themselves from their thoughts) (Assaz *et al.*, 2022). As such, for the purposes of this clinician-based guide, we acknowledge cognitive defusion primarily as an outcome; however, the focus of our interest is on outlining the ACT exercises that promote cognitive defusion.

To help explain cognitive defusion further, let us think about words: at their basic level, they are simply marks on a page or sounds spoken. If we think of a time when we have either seen or heard another language that we are unfamiliar with, then we have had an experience of words as just noises or scratches on a piece of paper or digital device. Nevertheless, in a language we understand, words can have tremendous significance. They can be merely descriptive, or they can be evaluative. Think of the following phrase: 'He is a tall man; he is a scary man.' A range of images and thoughts about the person might stem just from this phrase, and lead to a set of judgements and behaviours towards the man. Assumptions about the man might vary from person to person. While words have enabled humans to have advantages on this planet – such as the ability to categorise, analyse and be creative – they also have the power to make us judge others, ourselves and the world around us.

Words can have a powerful impact on our wellbeing, especially when they are applied to us in a critical and harsh manner. An early method to enable us to remove the power of words was researched by Severance and Washburn (1907) and later termed as 'semantic satiation' by Jakobovits and Lambert (1961). This method, used in ACT to bring about cognitive defusion, is where a word is repeated over and over so that it starts to lose its meaning and becomes merely a set of sounds. This idea formed the basis of the well-known exercise 'milk, milk, milk' (Masuda *et al.*, 2009; Titchener, 1916). This is where clients are taught how repeating a word that captures a difficult and evaluative thought can remove its emotional salience, thus creating distance and defusion from the thought (see Worksheet 3 provided in the resources at the end of this chapter).

The semantic satiation technique described above is just one of a range of methods to help bring about cognitive defusion. These methods can help reduce the unwanted impact from thoughts rather than changing their form or frequency (Kangas & McDonald, 2011). The therapeutic work involves opening up to the thought and making room for it, and becoming more mindful of thoughts by letting them come and go without attempting to focus on or avoid them. If we can disentangle from our thoughts, then it can open up space to engage in valued-driven behaviour (Rauwenhoff *et al.*, 2021).

Importance of cognitive defusion for people with neurological conditions

Living with a neurological condition (NC) can be challenging, hence there are several reasons why pwNCs could be prone to fusing with their thoughts, images and memories. This section will focus on neurocognitive changes and cognitive-emotional impacts.

Neurocognitive changes often occur as a result of NCs. Executive functioning difficulties are especially common and can affect the ability to organise thoughts and solve problems. Executive functioning difficulties can mean that a person may struggle to self-monitor, shift their cognitive set and switch attention. Hence problems with executive functioning can often lead to a rigid and inflexible thinking style. Moreover, changes to social cognition, such as being able to step outside one's own perspective to see a situation from someone else's point of view, can be challenging. Reduced self-awareness and loss of insight may also predispose those affected to fuse with their thoughts and be less able to make room for alternative perspectives.

Further to the neurocognitive changes, the cognitive-emotional impacts of living with an NC may also engender cognitive fusion. Living with an NC can mean that individuals' lives are turned upside down, leading people to have to cope with strong cognitive-emotional reactions. Cognitive-emotional reactions may arise as a direct consequence of the NC itself, with emotional regulation difficulties being a common issue following injury or disease in the brain. Furthermore, strong cognitive-emotional responses may result from the psychosocial changes of living with an NC, such as grief related to valued premorbid aspects of self, fear of future deterioration or recurrence, and adjusting one's life to a long-term condition, all of which may be a difficult process to accept (Kangas & McDonald, 2011; McLeod, 2015). Following a diagnosis of an NC, with a future often fraught with uncertainty, psychological difficulties involving challenging thoughts and feelings are common (e.g. anxiety, low mood, shame, anger, internalised stigma) (Nègre-Pagès *et al.*, 2010; Reijnders *et al.*, 2008).

These cognitive-emotional experiences may interrelate with dominant and oppressive problem-saturated discourses regarding pwNCs. Furthermore, oppression experienced by pwNCs may intersect with existing aspects of their identity and lived experience (e.g. gender, race, ability, age, religion, nationality, sexuality). Oppressive aspects of social context and resultant lived cognitive-emotional experiences may generate distress for pwNCs. The thoughts and feelings pwNCs experience can be powerful, and therefore practising exercises to defuse from them may be a real challenge. In our work with experts-by-experience affected by HD, they described that while techniques aimed to bring about defusion were helpful, it was necessary first to ensure that injustice and associated pain could be voiced, heard and adequately acknowledged. Without this, tools for cognitive defusion may feel aversive, as though they are, in some way, endorsing injustice. Techniques for cognitive defusion should not be used to dismiss the reality of oppression and marginalisation faced by pwNCs, nor to invalidate suffering associated with this. With a stance of solidarity and compassion from practitioners, tools for cognitive defusion can help navigate the impact of oppressive social contexts and challenging aspects of neurological conditions.

Living with the life-altering challenges of a neurological condition, especially when combined with disabling social circumstances, can understandably lead to feeling overwhelmed by distressing thoughts and narratives. Changing the content of thoughts may not always feel as relevant and helpful for pwNCs, particularly when thoughts are rational and balanced in the context of living with an NC. Yet such thoughts may have unhelpful or upsetting consequences which prevent people from living as well as possible with an NC. For instance, in progressive NCs, it is natural to have thoughts about the anticipated loss of abilities. However, dwelling on these thoughts can increase distress and create a sense of disconnection from one's values and experiences in the present. Methods to enhance cognitive defusion can be helpful here by acknowledging such thoughts, while adjusting the relationship to them through creating distance. This cannot stop the pain of living with an NC, but it can help reduce the additional suffering and loss that can arise when our mind is overwhelmed by such thoughts. Consequently, techniques for cognitive defusion can be beneficial for pwNCs by reducing overall distress (including moods described as depressive), while increasing psychological flexibility (Hill *et al.*, 2017).

What evidence is there for use of techniques that aid cognitive defusion among neurological populations?

Research examining the effectiveness of ACT among people with neurological conditions is in its infancy, therefore few studies have focused specifically on the techniques for cognitive defusion among this group. Theoretically, Rauwenhoff *et al.* (2021) argued that among people adapting to acquired brain injuries, thoughts which may be distressing also hold some truth and, in light of this, creating distance via defusion methods may be more relevant and appropriate than challenging such thoughts. Empirically, using exercises for cognitive defusion, which help view distressing thoughts differently, has been useful for people with epilepsy (Lundgren *et al.*, 2006). Taking a different perspective could shift experiences of thoughts among this group, including fearful thoughts of future seizures. Empirical evidence has also supported considering cognitive defusion as a therapeutic outcome for progressive NCs, namely multiple sclerosis (MS). Following a resilience training programme, 52 per cent of participants in Giovanetti *et al.*'s (2020) study reported being 'much more able to defuse from distressing thoughts and emotions'. They went on to say that these were a 'part of my life, but they no longer control or distress me as they used to'.

The effectiveness of ACT for pwNCs, however, is still uncertain, with one study of ACT for people with MS evidencing improvement in cognitive defusion for some participants, yet limited evidence of statistically significant improvement. Examining the broader literature on the use of 'cognitive defusion techniques' for pwNCs, Assaz *et al.* (2018) found that these techniques have been associated with positive outcomes on measures of emotional discomfort and believability of thoughts, and reductions in escape or avoidance behaviour, all of which may be of benefit to those living with NCs. As 'cognitive defusion exercises' tend to be included as part of complex interventions, their specific role in improving outcomes for people has not been well researched. However, there is the theoretical rationale for these methods to be helpful, supported by preliminary empirical evidence, and encouragement to offer this as an option for pwNCs if it sounds as if it may be helpful for them.

Adaptations of 'cognitive defusion techniques' for people with neurological conditions

Before we progress to the techniques we can use, we will first consider how the methods might need to be adapted to suit the needs of pwNCs. First, a person might have experienced cognitive changes, resulting in some exercises being difficult to understand or undertake if not adapted to their needs. For example, asking someone who has difficulty with expressive language or dysphasia to repeat aloud a thought (such as in the 'milk, milk, milk' technique described earlier and found in Worksheet 3) could be an exercise in frustration for them.

Second, pwNCs often have associated physical disabilities. This could mean that tasks involving motor skills might need to be changed to suit them; for example, the thoughts as hands metaphor (see Worksheet 9) may need to be acted out by the therapist, rather than asking the client to do it.

Third, and linked to the previous point, is the need for the practitioner to be sensitive to the life circumstances of the individual and how their condition might impact them now and in the future. Certain themes within traditional exercises for cognitive defusion could potentially be insensitive or inappropriate for the person, especially if grappling with adjusting to the loss of a skill, ability or role that was important to them. For example, we have provided a worksheet involving kicking a rugby ball or playing a sport (see Worksheet 1). While this might be well suited to some of the people we work with, others could find this difficult emotionally and another example (such as balloons floating; see Worksheet 6) might work better. Similarly, some exercises might involve thinking about issues that are sensitive to those affected by an NC; for example, the topic of old age could be unsuitable for someone with a life-limiting condition, or the topic of having children could be distressing for those living with genetic conditions such as HD or familial motor neurone disease.

Introducing cognitive defusion to our clients

It can be challenging to introduce the topic of cognitive defusion to our clients, and the suggestions made in this section have been largely influenced by John Blackledge's excellent 2015 book *Cognitive Defusion in Practice: A Clinician's Guide to Assessing, Observing & Supporting Change in Your Client.*

'Defusion techniques' can feel awkward or clunky to introduce into a session, and the timing of introducing the idea is important. It may not be appropriate to introduce techniques shortly after meeting someone. For example, asking someone who is adjusting to the life-changing situation of an NC to sing their thought or repeat a painful thought (think of the 'milk, milk, milk' exercise described earlier) on a first session is likely to invalidate their experiences and lead to them not wishing to return for another session. The same is true for psychological therapies in general: engagement and the development of an empathic therapeutic relationship is key. Nevertheless, subtle techniques can be used early on during therapeutic contact. Blackledge (2015) outlines how using 'mind' and 'thought' language conventions can be introduced to convey the idea that we are not our thoughts. This type of dialogue can gently be weaved into the conversation as is suggested in the following example assessment session:

Client: When I am with my wider family, and the grandkids come over, I want to be able to pick them up and play with them like I used to, but my body won't let me. Instead, they are having to wait on me and bring me drinks and so on. I just feel so useless.

Therapist: That's such a tough thought to have, that you feel useless. What other thoughts show up at those times?

Client: Well, I just feel like I'm spoiling everyone's day by not joining in.

Therapist: It must be really difficult, when your mind is telling you that you're spoiling the family time together. How do you cope at those times?

Client: Sometimes I just want to shut myself away. I make my excuses and go to my room.

Therapist: I'm sorry to hear that. It sounds as if then you miss out on the family time that is so meaningful for you.

While this technique can be a useful starting point, it is important not to overdo it. A constant reference to 'your thoughts' and 'your mind telling you' could lead to a less empathic style, potentially threatening the therapeutic connection that is a crucial aspect of therapy. Judicious use of labelling 'thoughts as thoughts' can be adopted for the 'hot' thoughts that appear to cause distress. Empathising with their situation, as well as using some of this language, can help to sow some seeds that can be built on gradually.

An ideal time to introduce further ideas about fusion and defusion is if the client raises a time when they realise that they can't rely on their thoughts as always being accurate. This can be shown in the following example:

Client: Over the past week my anxiety was really getting to me. I couldn't find my glasses and I was convinced I'd left them at the GP surgery. My wife said that I hadn't taken them to the surgery, but I was certain I had. She said I'd lost them before we left, but I can't remember that. I kept asking her to drive me back to look for them, and my anxiety was increasing. Well eventually, it turns out they were underneath my magazine at home.

Therapist: So, in that instance, your mind was convinced that they were at the surgery, but you later found out that your glasses were indeed at home? Sometimes our minds do that, they convince us that something is entirely true, but then we find out it isn't. Have you noticed other times when that is the case?

Client: Yes, I guess it has happened before. I once thought my wife had forgotten we were supposed to be going out for lunch – and I felt extremely let down by her – but it turns out she had made a booking and was going to surprise me.

Therapist: Our minds can be quite powerful at times, telling us that things are true when they may not be, especially when we are feeling stressed or anxious. It can happen in many situations, and I know it happens to me too, that our minds might be convincing us that something is true and we cannot step away and see them simply as thoughts. We can end up trusting our minds to be accurate when, in fact, our thoughts might not correspond to reality at all.

Client: Yes. I think you could be right...

Therapist: If you are open to the idea that our thoughts aren't always accurate, in future sessions, would you be willing to explore further thoughts that show up when you feel anxious and to consider ways of stepping back from them?

In this scenario, the therapist has asked permission to return to situations where defusion techniques could be further developed. If the client has memory problems, as is often the case with people experiencing NCs, the therapist may agree with the client for either of them to jot down some summary notes of the discussion. In this example, the therapist has also used an open and non-stigmatising approach by sharing that they too experience this and that it is common for all people. This can help validate the client and reduce any defensiveness on their part, especially for people who might be very rigid in their thinking.

If the foundations are laid, and the therapeutic relationship has developed such that the client appears open to the methods, further exercises for defusion can be introduced. An example conversation is provided below:

Therapist: One aim of ACT is to share skills that can enable us to carry painful thoughts and feelings without them having such a powerful influence and impact on us. We know that attempts to avoid or push away our painful thoughts can end up making things worse by making those things the focus of our efforts and attention. Instead, learning to observe our thoughts can help us to notice them as they are – just as thoughts and not facts. This can help us to gain some distance from our thoughts and let them go when they are unhelpful to us.

Client: Okay, that sounds interesting. I tell myself that I'm being stupid when I have a thought such as 'I'm useless'. I know I'm not entirely useless, but I feel that way all the time, so I try to change the way I think and say to myself, 'You are not useless', but I don't feel convinced as I am not able to do the things to support my family that I once was able to do.

Therapist: That sounds very difficult. It seems as if you get into a struggle, and by battling this thought, it uses a lot of energy and leads to feelings that somehow you are not acceptable. In ACT we have a different approach, so if the thought 'I'm useless' pops up, instead of trying to change this, or ignore it, we might instead use a variety of ways to help us create some distance from the thought and take its power away. Would you be willing to give these techniques a try?

An important factor to note when starting out with defusion-promoting techniques is that we (as therapists) might feel attuned to some methods more than others. If we do not feel convinced or feel awkward describing a method, the likelihood is that our clients will pick up on that and feel awkward or not invested too. Also, while we might be keen on certain techniques, it helps to be open to the idea that our clients may not share our enthusiasm for a specific method. We now turn to more discussion of the various techniques that can be used.

Useful metaphors to introduce the idea of defusion

Further to the scripts given above, there are several metaphors that can be used to help introduce the idea of defusion. One of these is the well-known 'passengers on the bus' (see Worksheet 7), which compares thoughts and feelings to passengers on a bus we are driving. The thoughts or 'passengers' can either steer you away from the destination you desire or help you arrive at a life you love. This metaphor blends well with other facets of the hexaflex, such as willingness and values.

Another metaphor that can assist with introducing defusion is 'computer programming' (Blackledge, 2015). This compares our problematic thoughts to output from a computer. Like a computer, our past experiences have 'programmed' us to have certain thoughts and these are simply churned out in response to that programming and do not necessarily reflect 'the truth'.

A further technique that can help introduce cognitive defusion is the metaphor of 'looking at thoughts as thoughts, rather than through thoughts' (Hayes, Strosahl & Wilson, 2011). This can be undertaken in a literal sense using coloured goggles, where the client is asked to put them on and see the world as a specific shade. The goggles can then be compared to the difficult thoughts we have and how they 'colour' our world view. Therefore, we might say we are looking through our 'angry goggles' or our 'anxious goggles' when certain thoughts show up.

Finally, the bad cup metaphor described in the next section is a method that can be used to help explain the difference between descriptive language and evaluations, and can be useful in the earlier stages of discussing fusion and defusion.

Techniques for cognitive defusion

In this section, we will look at the six ways to enhance cognitive defusion, including: playing, questioning, actions, observing, responding and objectification (Assaz *et al.*, 2018). Consistent with the example scripts above, before practising these techniques, make sure to first acknowledge the client's inner experiences, validate the impact that they can have, provide the opportunity to practise the technique as an optional invitation, and gain permission to try the technique.

Playing

We can practise defusion through playing with the words that hook us, by stealing our attention and controlling our behaviour. With a client, pick one of these 'hot' thoughts – it might be a word or phrase – and recommend that they play with it. This technique would not be suitable for individuals with compromised language or speech skills. It could also be inappropriate for people who are affected by perseveration and find it difficult to switch attention.

Examples of playing with a hot thought include:

- Saying it aloud repeatedly (e.g. 'useless, useless, useless, useless, useless').
- Saying it with a silly or funny voice (e.g. like a cartoon character, or by changing the pitch).
- Changing the pace by speaking rapidly like a mouse, or slowly like a whale.
- Singing the thought (e.g. try singing in an operatic way, or to a dance song).
- Saying a translation (e.g. a synonym in another language, even a fictional one like Klingon).

Playing with words, and Titchener's (1916) 'milk, milk, milk' repetition in particular, is a well-known method of removing the feeling of meaning that words can hold. Playing with words can be a useful method to start with.

Questioning

These techniques focus on questioning the coherence of the reasons and stories we hold, for example questioning the causes of our behaviour. We often hold these reasons and stories without realising them, so these techniques involve finding as well as questioning these reasons and stories.

Here are some examples:

- Picking a behaviour and repeatedly answering 'why?' until no reason remains.
- Creating a new story, by writing the story of their life and altering the outcome for themselves now.
- Listing all the characteristics they would define themselves by, noticing the ones that don't match or contradict one another, and letting go of these words.

While these questioning techniques may resonate with some of our clients, some caution might be needed for some people. The method of creating a new story with a different ending could potentially engender feelings of sadness for someone struggling to adjust to life with an NC, or even unrealistic expectations for someone who lacks self-awareness. If the client has difficulties with generating ideas, this also might not be the most suitable technique. Some people could be offered support with writing out the story or you might read it out for them. As with all techniques, the therapeutic relationship is paramount, and permission to try such an approach should be gained.

Actions

This group of defusion practices support us in experiencing the difference between thoughts and actions by disrupting thought-action fusion. As with other 'defusion techniques', consideration of which actions to choose should be based on knowing the person with an NC and what their abilities are. For example, it would be highly inappropriate for someone who uses a wheelchair to be given the 'I can't walk' exercise that is described below.

Here are some examples of action-based techniques:

- Separating causes of behaviour from thoughts and feelings by picking a physical action (e.g. filling a glass with water), recommending that they convince themselves not to do the action, and then do it.

- Writing an action on a card (e.g. I can't sing, I can't walk) and holding the card while doing the action.

The above techniques provide examples that illustrate how our inner worlds may think or feel something as factual, but this does not necessarily mean they are, and our actions can be independent from them. Let us take, for example, a hot thought such as 'I won't have any friends because I have had a stroke' or 'I will never enjoy painting again now I have a brain tumour'. Such thoughts can generate distress which is very real, but it does not mean the prediction is true nor that one's behaviours must be limited by the thoughts or distress.

Observing

Observation-based practices for defusion involve attending to the responses, the inner experiences, that usually pass by unnoticed.

Here are some examples:

- Using visualisation exercises of placing thoughts onto objects and watching them pass by within the mind's eye (e.g. leaves floating along a stream, a parade of people with signs), or even patterns of thoughts and worries (e.g. worry as a freight train passing by a viewing platform).

- In real life settings, imagining placing thoughts onto objects that pass by such as clouds in the sky, cars on the street, or sushi on a sushi belt.

- For personalised practices, asking the client to recall a situation which stirred noticeable thoughts and feelings, then reflecting on the inner events this stirred (thoughts, predictions, sensations, emotions, urges, resistances, memories), and considering with them the part of themselves that is observing these inner experiences.

These observational exercises align well with mindfulness and meditation practices that clients may already be familiar with, or that can help nurture an observational stance towards their inner life. If the person with an NC has difficulties remembering what the task involves, then they could be supported through visual prompts or instructions, such as that provided in Worksheet 4. In our experience, even clients with significant neurocognitive difficulties have appeared to value being supported to undertake such mindfulness-based practices to help defuse from their distressing thoughts.

Responding

Once you have practised observations of thoughts, 'responding' methods involve supporting clients to tune in further to the different types of inner experiences, or relational responses, that can be stirred within us.

Here are some examples of these techniques:

- Acknowledging thoughts and inner experiences through labelling them by their categories (e.g. a thought, worry, comparison, memory).

- Building on labelling through noting practices within the mind or aloud by preceding a difficult thought with the words 'I'm having the thought that...' (e.g. 'I'm useless' becomes 'I'm having the thought that I'm useless').

- Reframing the validity of evaluations through the bad cup metaphor. Get a cup and discuss its material properties (e.g. colour, height, width), and then provide an evaluation (e.g. good, bad, beautiful, awful). Notice that the evaluations can shift from different perspectives, and no evaluation is truly in the cup, it's in the eye of the evaluator.

- Harnessing gratitude and being thankful for the thought (e.g. 'Thank you mind for alerting me to danger, but I am safe to walk with my frame').

These techniques can support clients to notice whether there are patterns of relational responses that arise more frequently than others. They can be practised 'live' in sessions or encouraged prospectively as a home-practice. They follow on well as an extension of the observational practices, building on from noticing to responding and can be incorporated into metacognitive rehabilitation techniques. Where speech or memory might be difficult for some people, they could be helped with written prompts (such as 'thoughts', 'memory' in the labelling exercise) and be given opportunities to point to or select the relevant inner experience.

Objectification

Thoughts and inner experiences are given physical properties and objectified to varying extents. These defusion-enhancing methods match closely with playful techniques and some of the more visual approaches to observation. To support in creating some distance and defusion through objectification, here are some example practices:

- Writing the words down (if possible for the person to do so).

- Discussing (or even drawing out and creating) some physical properties for thoughts. What size, shape, colour or texture might they have?

- Practising the 'thoughts as hands' metaphor (Worksheet 9). Here a client imagines the valued and challenging parts of their life, they hold their hands open as if reading a book and imagine that these are thoughts and feelings; they imagine becoming hooked by a thought or feeling and this means their hands now cover their eyes. Reflect together on what this means for them and their values.

- Practising the metaphor of the passengers on the bus. Herein our observing self is the driver of a bus, heading in the direction of a valued life. Different passengers arrive on the bus, representing thoughts and emotions which capture your attention. Consider how we might typically respond to them (e.g. struggling, arguing or fighting, giving in, or stopping). Discuss the possibility of acknowledging these inner experiences and choosing to continue in the direction of your values. A printable handout of the passengers on the bus metaphor is provided in the resources at the end of this chapter (Worksheet 7).

For clinicians new to ACT and cognitive defusion, it can be tricky deciding where to start with the various techniques. To aid our decisions, it can be helpful to reflect on the areas where the client is hoping to see change and to consider what tools or metaphors might best suit the client's preferences and abilities. Exercises might also be chosen according to the needs of the person in terms of where their strengths lie, such as whether they are able to move, speak, read and so on. A selection of worksheets to use with clients can be found in the resources at the end of this chapter.

CASE EXAMPLE

Mr A is a 46-year-old man with a clinical diagnosis of Huntington's disease (HD). He inherited HD from his father. As a child, Mr A experienced some bullying from peers at school as his father gave the appearance of being drunk, due to the motor difficulties associated with HD.

Mr A was referred to a psychological service for help with low mood, anxiety and difficulties managing his temper. On assessment, he described recurrent thoughts about how he was an embarrassment to his family. Mr A's partner considered Mr A not embarrassing at all, but rather overly self-critical. Mr A said he'd tried to challenge these thoughts, but the negative side always seemed to win out, resulting in him feeling more frustrated with himself. While struggling with frustration, Mr A would withdraw from spending time with his partner and with his friends, both of whom he valued deeply.

As part of an overall ACT approach, his psychologist gradually introduced the idea that thoughts are not reality and Mr A accepted this well. By using ACT to help formulate his difficulties, Mr A recognised that his sensitivity to being embarrassing was rooted in his experiences of being bullied as a child, and assumptions that he would follow a similar pattern to his father in being 'embarrassing'. The psychologist used the computer programming metaphor (Blackledge, 2015) to discuss this idea with Mr A. Instead of continuing with his 'thought challenging battles', Mr A was invited to consider other options to cope with his thoughts.

On exploring the different approaches for cognitive defusion, Mr A found that he particularly liked the noting technique of 'I'm having the thought that...'. He and his partner also started to use the 'embarrassment story' as a method of helping Mr A to defuse from his distressing thoughts. Mr A commented that he felt more able to observe and notice his thoughts. With his thoughts starting to feel less intense and powerful, Mr A found he had more space to focus on what mattered most to him.

Summary and conclusion

In this chapter, we discussed what is meant by cognitive fusion and defusion. We explored the significance of words and how cognitive defusion can be facilitated when words (and subsequently thoughts) lose their power. We examined why pwNCs may be especially prone to experiencing cognitive fusion due to brain changes affecting cognitive functioning and emotional regulation skills, and also how the life-changing situation of an NC can engender a range of psychological difficulties. We looked at why techniques for cognitive defusion might offer some benefits for pwNCs over cognitive restructuring used in traditional cognitive behaviour therapy. We discussed how there is a paucity of studies that explore cognitive defusion among pwNCs and there is much work to do in this area. Further to this, we provided some suggestions for how methods to promote cognitive defusion can be adapted for pwNCs, taking into account their cognitive and physical difficulties, and applying sensitivity to the changes in identity that can occur as a result of an NC. We discussed the importance of how cognitive defusion is introduced to our clients, to help maintain therapeutic engagement. Finally, we gave an overview of the range of methods that can be used, described a case example and, in the resources at the end of the chapter, have provided a set of worksheets to be used with clients. We hope that this chapter has provided some useful information to help clinicians support pwNCs to cope with the challenges of difficult and upsetting thoughts that can understandably arise from living with a NC.

References

Assaz, D. A., Roche, B., Kanter, J. W. & Oshiro, C. K. (2018). Cognitive defusion in acceptance and commitment therapy: What are the basic processes of change? *The Psychological Record*, 68(4), 405–418.

Assaz, D. A., Tyndall, I., Oshiro, C. K. & Roche, B. (2022). A process-based analysis of cognitive defusion in Acceptance and Commitment Therapy. *Behavior Therapy*, 54(6), 1020–1035.

Blackledge, J. T. (2015). *Cognitive Defusion in Practice: A Clinician's Guide to Assessing, Observing & Supporting Change in Your Client*. Oakland, CA: New Harbinger Publications.

Dale, M., Eccles, F. J. R., Melvin, K., Khan, Z. *et al.* (2023). Guided self-help for anxiety among Huntington's disease gene expansion carriers (GUIDE-HD) compared to treatment as usual: A randomised controlled feasibility trial. *Pilot and Feasibility Studies*, 12(1), 159.

De Houwer, J., Barnes-Holmes, Y. & Barnes-Holmes, D. (2016). Riding the waves: A functional-cognitive perspective on the relations among behaviour therapy, cognitive behaviour therapy and acceptance and commitment therapy. *International Journal of Psychology*, 51(1), 40–44.

Giovannetti, A. M., Quintas, R., Tramacere, I., Giordano, A. *et al.* (2020). A resilience group training program for people with multiple sclerosis: Results of a pilot single-blind randomized controlled trial and nested qualitative study. *PloS One*, 15(4), e0231380.

Hayes, S. C., Strosahl, K. D. & Wilson, K. G. (2011). *Acceptance and Commitment Therapy: The Process and Practice of Mindful Change*. New York, NY: Guilford Press.

Hill, G., Hynd, N., Wheeler, M., Tarran-Jones, A., Carrabine, H. & Evans, S. (2017). Living well with neurological conditions: Evaluation of an ACT-informed group intervention for psychological adjustment in outpatients with neurological problems. *The Neuropsychologist*, 3, 58–63.

Jakobovits, L. A. & Lambert, W. E. (1961). Semantic satiation among bilinguals. *Journal of Experimental Psychology*, 62(6), 576.

Kangas, M. & McDonald, S. (2011). Is it time to act? The potential of acceptance and commitment therapy for psychological problems following acquired brain injury. *Neuropsychological Rehabilitation*, 21(2), 250–276.

Lundgren, T., Dahl, J., Melin, L. & Kies, B. (2006). Evaluation of acceptance and commitment therapy for drug refractory epilepsy: A randomized controlled trial in South Africa—a pilot study. *Epilepsia*, 47(12), 2173–2179.

Masuda, A., Hayes, S. C., Twohig, M. P., Drossel, C., Lillis, J. & Washio, Y. (2009). A parametric study of cognitive defusion and the believability and discomfort of negative self-relevant thoughts. *Behavior Modification*, 33(2), 250–262.

McEnteggart, C., Barnes-Holmes, Y., Hussey, I. & Barnes-Holmes, D. (2015). The ties between a basic science of language and cognition and clinical applications. *Current Opinion in Psychology*, 2, 56–59.

McLeod, H. J. (2015). Acceptance and commitment therapy's value as a neuropsychotherapy. *The Neuropsychologist*, 1, 14–15.

Nègre-Pagès, L., Grandjean, H., Lapeyre-Mestre, M., Montastruc, J. L. *et al.* (2010). Anxious and depressive symptoms in Parkinson's disease: The French cross-sectional DoPaMiP study. *Movement Disorders*, 25(2), 157–166.

Rauwenhoff, J., Peeters, F., Bol, Y. & Van Heugten, C. (2021). Measuring psychological flexibility and cognitive defusion in individuals with acquired brain injury. *Brain Injury*, 35(10), 1301–1307.

Reijnders, J. S., Ehrt, U., Weber, W. E., Aarsland, D. & Leentjens, A. F. (2008). A systematic review of prevalence studies of depression in Parkinson's disease. *Movement Disorders*, 23(2), 183–189.

Severance, E. & Washburn, M. F. (1907). The loss of associative power in words after long fixation. *The American Journal of Psychology*, 182–186.

Titchener, E. B. (1916). *A Text-book of Psychology*. New York, NY: Macmillan.

Converting Your Thoughts

Adapted from 'Kicking soccer balls' by John Robert-Clyde Helmer (2013).

This exercise best suits people who have a keen interest in sports. It can be easily modified to reflect your sporting preference.

If you want to, close your eyes and take a moment to find a comfortable position, and allow your breath to find its natural rhythm.

- Picture yourself on a rugby pitch, standing in front of the goalposts.

- Next to you is a pile of rugby balls. Take a moment to imagine the scene.

- As you reach down for the first ball, imagine putting one of your distressing thoughts onto the ball.

- When you can imagine that thought clearly on the ball, put the ball on the kicking tee, keeping focus on the thought, as you prepare to run up and kick it.

- Now run up to the ball and kick the thought off into the distance, watching it sail in between the posts.

- As you watch the ball travel off into the distance, take another deep breath.

- Now return to the pile of balls and do this with another ball and another thought.

- It might be the same thought as before, and that is okay, or you might notice it is a different thought.

This technique can be adapted to whatever sport you are most familiar with – for example, it could be hitting a golf ball from a tee or kicking a football down a pitch.

Pushing Away Paper

Exercise by Dr Russ Harris.

- Imagine all that is in front of you is everything that matters most to you, as well as your daily tasks and any problems or challenges you have to face.

- Now imagine that the paper on your lap represents all the problematic thoughts, feelings and emotions you want to get rid of.

- Begin by holding the piece of paper tightly on either side, then stretch out your arms keeping the paper at arm's length.

- This is getting the negative thoughts and feelings as far away from you as possible.

- Try and notice three things as you hold the paper in front of you.

- First, notice how tiring it is to hold the paper; think how this would feel after a day.

- Second, notice how distracting it is, if someone was in front of you trying to talk, it would be very difficult to concentrate on them.

- Third, notice how hard it is to take action and do things you love to do when all your energy goes into holding the paper.

- So, notice how difficult life is when you're struggling with your thoughts and feelings like this. You're distracted, you're missing out on life.

- Now lower the paper and place it on your lap. Notice how much more energy you have, how less tired you are and the ease of concentrating on what is in front of you.

- Notice that the paper is still with you, you have not got rid of it, you have instead found a new way to interact with it.

- It might be that the thoughts and feelings can be useful in some way, and although uncomfortable, might be trying to help you.

Milk, Milk, Milk!

Exercise by Dr Akihiko Masuda and colleagues (2009).

This exercise aims to remove the emotional impact, believability and discomfort of strong negative self-referential words.

- Start by finding yourself a comfortable environment in which you will not be disturbed.

- Think about the word 'milk', noting what images or other words spring to mind.

- As a first exercise, begin by repeating the word 'milk' out loud over and over again for 45 seconds.

- After 45 seconds, take note of any association with the word 'milk' now. Has it become just a meaningless sound?

- Now think of a word that has a strong negative self-referential quality for you.

- As before, notice what feelings, emotions and thoughts come up when you think of this word.

- Now complete the first exercise again but this time repeat the word you are currently thinking of.

- Remember to say the word out loud.

- After 45 seconds, take note of any association with the word now.

- This is something you can repeat on a daily basis, and soon the word will lose all meaning.

Leaves on a Stream

Exercise by Dr Steven Hayes.

- Get yourself in a comfortable position, allowing your eyes to close if you want.

- Visualise yourself sitting beside a gently flowing stream with leaves floating along the surface of the water.

- Now, with every thought that enters your mind, picture yourself placing it on one of the leaves and letting it float by.

- Don't worry if you find yourself without thoughts, just continue watching the stream and the leaves floating down it.

- Try to let the leaves pass at their own pace. It is easy to try and get rid of the thoughts by visualising the leaves moving quickly, but just relax and allow them to pass naturally.

- You might have negative thoughts about the exercise, but just like all other thoughts, place those on a leaf, and let them pass.

- If a leaf gets stuck, allow it to hang around until it is ready to float by. If the thought comes up again, watch it float by another time.

- If a difficult or painful feeling arises, simply acknowledge it. Say to yourself, 'I notice myself having these feelings.' Place those thoughts on leaves and allow them to float along.

- Allow the image of the stream to dissolve and slowly bring your attention back to your surroundings.

The Sushi Train

Adapted from Reyelle McKeever.

- Imagine yourself sitting in a Sushi restaurant, watching the sushi train going around. All the dishes on the train are created by the chef.

- The chef is like our minds, and the dishes they create are like the thoughts that crop up throughout the day.

- When you look at all the dishes that go by on the sushi train, you notice that they are all different – some of them look delicious, and others look rancid.

- These are like our thoughts: some are pleasant, and we want to keep hold of them; others are negative, and we want to avoid them; and some can just be neutral and not bring on any feelings.

- As the day goes on, the chef of our mind continues to create lots of different dishes, all of which go onto the sushi train and continue going round and round in our minds.

- Now just allow the dishes to go around on the train; you don't have to reach out for the delicious food, nor turn away from the rancid food, you can just let them pass by.

- You can do the same with your thoughts. You do not have to hold on to the pleasant thoughts or hide away from the horrible ones, you can just watch them pass by in your mind.

Letting Go of a Balloon

Adapted from Dr Steven Hayes.

- Start by finding yourself a comfortable environment where you will not be disturbed.

- Imagine yourself in a calm and peaceful outside space. Next to you is a bunch of balloons, all of them are different colours, shapes and sizes.

- Imagine picking up one of the balloons, and when you look at it, imagine your distressing thought written on it.

- Now hold the balloon by your side, and when you feel ready, let go of the balloon.

- Notice the balloon float away into the distance, and how you feel when you watch it float away.

- When the balloon is no longer in sight, take another balloon from the bunch.

- Again, imagine a distressing thought written on the balloon. It might be the same thought but that is okay.

- Follow the same process of holding the balloon by your side, and when you are feeling ready, let go of the balloon and watch it float away into the distance.

Passengers on the Bus

Exercise by Hayes et al. *1999.*

- Imagine yourself as a bus driver, going on the journey that is life. You are trying to drive towards a place which you value.

- However, throughout the journey passengers come aboard the bus, bringing with them thoughts, feelings and emotions.

- Some of the passengers you like, as they bring with them happy thoughts, but some of the passengers you dislike, as they bring with them scary thoughts and negative memories.

- You just have to keep driving. Unfortunately, the difficult passengers may block your view, shout out or point out potential dangers.

- When this happens, you might feel like arguing with the passengers, and this is in turn means stopping the bus and prevents you moving forward.

- You might feel it wise to listen to the passengers and allow them to dictate the direction of the bus. Although this might initially feel easier, you would be steering away from your values.

- What is important to remember is that all passengers will come and go throughout the journey; some may stay for long periods whereas some might get off quickly. However, they all got on the bus knowing the destination, so where they want to go is the right place.

- You should acknowledge all the passengers that get on your bus, but throughout the journey, you are the one that is in control, regardless of what the passengers say.

The Mind Monster

Adapted from Hayes et al. 1999.

Sometimes we can think of our anxieties and depressive thoughts as a monster within our minds. It can seem very strong and big and at times overwhelming.

This monster says very upsetting things and works against us, pulling a length of rope into a pit full of our fears and despairs. When we engage with the monster, we begin to pull back on the rope. This tug-of-war is constant and exhausting. The harder we pull, the harder the monster pulls.

We feed the monster and make it even bigger and stronger, by pulling harder on the rope, by listening and paying attention to the monster, by believing the monster, and by reacting to the monster – by how we feel and what we do.

If we could let go of the rope, what would happen?

The monster would still be there, saying what it says, but it would have no power to pull us towards the great pit. As we stop feeding it, gradually it will get weaker, smaller and quieter.

Hands as Thoughts and Feelings

Adapted from Dr Russ Harris.

- Imagine that out there in front of you is everything that really matters to you, everything that makes your life meaningful, all the people, places and activities you love, all the things you like to do. But that's not all. Also, there are all the problems and challenges you need to deal with in your life today, and all the tasks you need to do on a regular basis to make your life work, such as shopping, cooking, cleaning, driving, doing your tax return and so on.

- Imagine that your hands are your thoughts and feelings. Now, let's see what happens when you allow them to cloud your vision.

- Raise your open palms in front of your face. Notice three things. First, how much are you missing out on right now? How disconnected and disengaged are you from the people and things that matter? Second, how difficult is it to focus your attention on what you need to do? If there's an important task in front of you right now, how hard is it to focus on it? Third, notice how difficult it is, like this, to take action, to do the things that make your life work. So notice how difficult life is when you're hooked. You're missing out, you're cut off and disconnected.

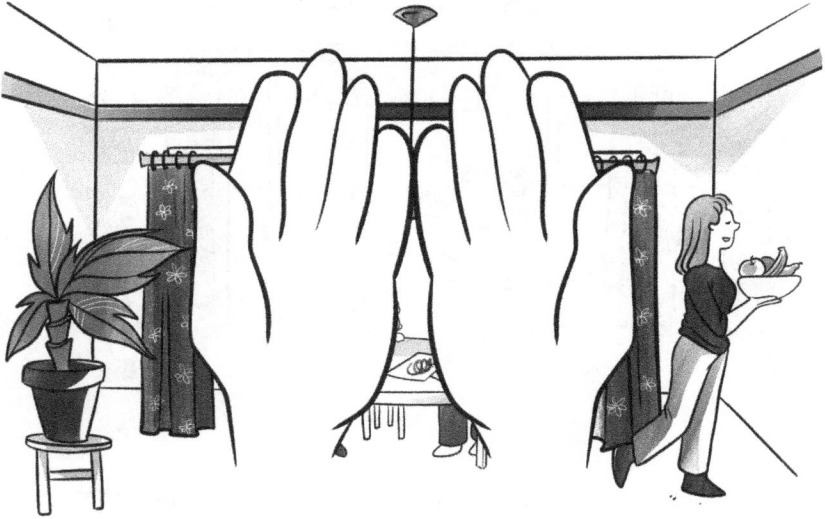

- Now, let's see what happens when you lower your hands. What's your view of the room like now? How much easier is it to engage and connect? If there's a task you need to do, how much easier is it to focus on it?

- Move your arms and hands about. How much easier is it now to take action? Your hands haven't disappeared, they're still here. So, if there's something useful you can do with them, you can use them. Even really painful thoughts and feelings often have useful information that can help you, even if it's just pointing you towards problems you need to address or things you need to do differently.

If there's nothing useful you can do with them, you just let them sit there.

References

Harris, R. (2002). *ACT Made Simple: An Easy-to-Read Primer on Acceptance and Commitment Therapy* (second edition). Oakland, CA: New Harbinger Publications.

Harris, R. (2019). *ACT made simple: an easy to read primer on ACT* (2nd Ed.). Oakland CA: New Harbinger Publications.

Harris, R. (2023). Pushing away paper. In R. Harris. *ACT made Simple: an easy to read primer on ACT.* (2nd Ed.). (pp. 104–105). New Harbinger Publications.

Hayes, S. C. Leaves on a stream. In S. C. Hayes, K. Strosahl & K. G. Wilson. (1999). *Acceptance and Commitment Therapy: An Experiential Approach to Behavior Change.* New York, NY: Guilford Press.

Hayes, S. C., Strosahl, K. & Wilson, K. G. (1999). *Acceptance and Commitment Therapy: An Experiential Approach to Behavior Change.* New York, NY: Guilford Press.

Helmer, J. R. C. (2013). Kicking soccer balls. In S. C. Hayes, J. A. Afari (Eds). *The big book of ACT metaphors: a practitioner guide to experiential exercises & metaphors in ACT.* (pp. 69–70). Oakland, CA: New Harbinger Publications.

Masuda, A., Hayes, S. C., Twohig, M. P., Drossel, C., Lillis, J., & Washio, Y. (2009). A parametric study of cognitive defusion and the believability and discomfort of negative self-relevant thoughts. *Behavior Modification*, 33(2), 250–262.

McKeever, R. (2016). *Sushi Train Metaphor.* www.actcursus.nl/wp-content/uploads/2017/04/Sushi-Train-metaphor-Reyelle-McKeever.pdf

Stoddard, J. A. & Afari, N. (2013). *The Big Book of ACT Metaphors: A Practitioner's Guide to Experiential Exercises and Metaphors in Acceptance and Commitment Therapy.* Oakland, CA: New Harbinger Publications.

CHAPTER 4

Present Moment Awareness in Acquired Brain Injury

LORRAINE KING, NATALIE HAMPSON AND EMILY BUNN

About the authors

Lorraine King is a consultant clinical neuropsychologist working in a large outpatient Clinical Neuropsychology service within North Staffordshire Combined Healthcare NHS Trust, and also in private practice. She specialises in traumatic brain injury (TBI), ranging from mild/post-concussion presentations to the more severe end of the TBI spectrum.

Natalie Hampson is a consultant clinical neuropsychologist who has been working in the acquired brain injury field for over 20 years and specialises in the assessment and treatment of people who have severe and complex difficulties as a result of their injuries. She currently works in private practice and in a slow stream brain injury rehabilitation unit managed by the Leonard Cheshire charity. Lorraine and Natalie previously worked together in community multidisciplinary neuro-rehabilitation services at Salford Royal NHS Foundation Trust.

Natalie and Lorraine both have a keen interest in applying acceptance and commitment therapy (ACT) with people who have neurological conditions, and with their families and care teams, and are also involved in several current research projects in this area. They have found the 'present moment awareness' (PMA) corner of the ACT hexaflex to be of particular value in these populations, specifically for people who are struggling with cognitive difficulties, such as attentional and behavioural control, in supporting them to learn more purposeful ways of directing attentional focus and responding to events. They have also found that PMA can be used as a concrete skill for people with more severe neurological injuries who may struggle to grasp some of the more abstract areas of the hexaflex. Given that PMA can help with this, it also offers a sense of self-efficacy and empowerment to individuals who may experience a lack of agency and control within their lives.

Emily Bunn is currently an assistant psychologist working with Lorraine in an NHS outpatient neuropsychology service at North Staffordshire Combined Healthcare NHS Trust where they are very much proponents of ACT. Emily has worked in the assessment and ongoing care of adults who have received a diagnosis of dementia for several years, and also with children and adults who have received a diagnosis of learning disability and/or autism. She is about to leave the service to embark on clinical psychology doctorate training at Lancaster University.

Introduction

In this chapter, we present an explanation of PMA and the research base for its use within neurological populations; one of Natalie's clinical cases for a rich example of real-world use; a table suggesting adaptations to traditional PMA techniques for people with acquired brain injury, for whom it might be difficult to access traditional practice; and a list of suggested resources.

The importance of being present for people with neurological conditions

Life is what happens to you while you're busy making other plans.
ALLEN SAUNDERS, AMERICAN WRITER, JOURNALIST AND CARTOONIST

Present moment awareness (PMA) is an important component of

ACT in people with acquired brain injury (ABI) because it encourages acceptance of thoughts, feelings and bodily sensations as they are experienced, as opposed to challenging or trying to get rid of them. This can be particularly helpful for people who have an ABI or live with a neurological condition, who can experience permanent changes in cognitive, physical or functional abilities beyond their control, alongside the difficult thoughts and feelings that inevitably arise from this (Kangas & McDonald, 2011).

One of the aims of ACT is to increase PMA and notice thoughts, feelings and sensations as they occur, experiencing thoughts non-judgementally and being open to what feelings may arise. From a place of acceptance, it is hoped that less focus will be placed on what cannot be changed and more space can be made for things that are important to us, that is, our values (Hayes, Strosahl & Wilson, 2012). Interoception involves awareness of internal bodily processes from the skin inwards, while exteroception involves understanding and interacting with external stimuli from within our environment. Being present involves utilising our senses to fully experience both our internal world, observing thoughts and feelings compassionately and promoting acceptance of suffering and adversity, and also the world around us as it is, noticing the here and now (e.g. smells, textures, sights, sounds, sensations and tastes), to increase awareness of and presence within this moment in our lives. This also seeks to stop our minds from wandering into the past and future (although being accepting when it inevitably does), gently and compassionately bringing it back to the target of focus.

PMA may be increased through practising mindfulness, including listening to guided meditation, bringing attention to an object, or through everyday activities, such as mindfully walking or eating. In ACT, thoughts are often seen as just thoughts, not facts. Though we may not be able to control what happens to us, we are able to consciously consider, notice or work on how we respond to happenings. We may experience pain or adverse life experiences, and understandably begin to think thoughts such as 'Why did this happen to me? Life will never be the same' and then begin to ruminate on these thoughts and feel anxious about the past and the future

(Detert, 2015). Engaging in mindfulness practice can help to decentre thoughts, allowing us to take a step back and review the helpfulness of these thoughts, and consider a more adaptive and creative way of responding. The more that mindfulness is practised, the more helpful it can be in naturally reducing psychological distress and increasing psychological flexibility (Harris, 2019). A psychologically flexible relationship with present moment experience is broadly suggested to be the foundation of effective executive function (Kashdan & Rottenberg, 2010).

Practising mindfulness or becoming aware of the present moment may be difficult for someone with an ABI, due to each individual's unique constellation of physical, cognitive, emotional and neurobehavioural changes, dependent on the site and extent of the injury (Rabinowitz & Levin, 2014). Thus, it may be difficult for a person with an ABI to sustain their attention while engaging in a mindfulness exercise or to bring their attention back to the present moment if it wanders. There could also be difficulties with understanding and retaining information during and after intervention, as well as initiating and remembering when and how to routinely practise skills. In addition, it is important to note that what is happening in the present moment may be daunting and unpleasant, for example if residing in a hospital setting (Smart, Curvis & Methley, 2021). In our own clinical practice, we seek to emphasise the benefits of PMA for maintaining attentional focus, improving mood and helping with impulse control after a neurological event. It feels important to 'sell' this way of working as sometimes our clients are sceptical about it being kooky/hippy, thus we would share this view, but invite them to try it with us, despite it feeling a bit odd, because it really is effective!

Understanding of ACT metaphors (e.g. Harris, 2019) requires abstract thinking, which may be difficult following an ABI if there are difficulties comprehending abstract concepts or more complex information. Further, potential sensory changes after an ABI may affect the ability to utilise senses to fully experience the present moment (King, 2021). Impairments in swallowing or mobility could inhibit participation in mindful eating/drinking/walking practice, or body scans. Post-acquired brain injury changes can often be lifelong and may require significant emotional adjustment.

Therefore, rehabilitation interventions and strategies for managing symptoms and deficits are vital for valued living. Despite the potential barriers highlighted above, PMA can be particularly beneficial for this population if creative adaptations are made, which is the bread and butter of neuro-rehabilitation practitioners. For example, a common sequelae of brain injury is reduced insight. Mindfulness practice can increase awareness, such as noticing if a body part is not moving effectively; becoming more aware of irritable thoughts, or feelings of inadequacy, and can thus improve insight (Hill *et al.*, 2017). Being able to recognise how you are feeling, or your present physical and emotional condition, can be a first step to acceptance. Unlike other therapies, such as cognitive behavioural therapy (CBT), inviting someone to think and feel what they naturally do in the here and now, without fighting or challenging it, reduces the risk of invalidating or dismissing very normal, understandable and human feelings in response to significant life events (Gregg *et al.*, 2007). PMA promotes acceptance of thoughts, feelings and bodily sensations as they occur. Other therapies that include thought challenging and identifying unhelpful thoughts and patterns of behaviour can require a degree of energy and attention which may not be available after an ABI. Allowing thoughts to come and go as they please releases us from this exhausting struggle, and frees up space in our minds to focus potentially limited attentional resources and energy on things that are important to us.

Research literature on PMA in neurological populations

There is increasing evidence to support the effectiveness of PMA strategies in different neurological conditions, with mindfulness-based interventions found to be acceptable and feasible for people following an ABI (e.g. Jani *et al.*, 2018; Niraj, Wright & Powell, 2020; Wang, Thiel & Graff, 2022; Wrapson *et al.*, 2021). For example, Lovette *et al.* (2022) conducted a scoping review of 29 studies primarily focused on mindfulness-based interventions for people with mild

TBI but also containing research with moderate-severe TBI. Results showed the domains of coping, somatisation, emotional symptoms and stress response were the most frequently improved, with the greatest effect sizes also observed in coping, emotional symptoms, stress response and specific subdomains of cognition, particularly attention and new learning. A recent scoping review of the literature by Mak *et al.* (2023) on the use of mindfulness-based interventions following stroke also identified 16 studies comprising group mindfulness-based stress reduction (MBSR) (Kabat-Zinn, 2003) and studies which adapted mindfulness into taster sessions or shorter durations and individual sessions to make interventions more suitable for people with concentration and fatigue difficulties. The review identified good evidence for the benefits of mindfulness for mental fatigue, aspects of cognition such as ability to focus attention, and quality of life, with mixed results for improvements in mood and physical functioning due to study limitations. They also highlighted that the frequency of standard MBSR is likely to be a barrier to people with ABI, but the issue of how mindfulness-based interventions should be tailored regarding frequency, duration and session content for individuals post-stroke requires further exploration.

To complement the growing literature on interoceptively focused PMA, there has also been an increased interest in the benefits of exteroceptive PMA, including the merits of the Japanese nature-based practice of 'forest bathing' (no actual bathing involved), which involves an immersive and sensory connection with nature (Kotera, Richardson & Sheffield, 2022; Song *et al.*, 2017; Yi, Seo & An, 2022). This may take the form of a slow, mindful walk through a forest or local park, but can also be practised at home with a plant or in a garden. Virtual forest bathing has also been shown to have beneficial effects for adults with physical disability and reduced mobility (McEwan *et al.*, 2023), so has likely benefits for use within ABI. Nature-based mindfulness in ABI is currently being researched and trialled clinically within a 'Neuro in Nature' social enterprise by Delaney and McDonald (2023) in the North West (UK).

PMA is also a key aspect of ACT interventions and there is increasing evidence to support the use of ACT incorporating PMA for treating psychological distress in people with ABI (Curvis & Methley, 2021). For example, Whiting *et al.* (2020) randomly assigned 19 individuals with a severe TBI to an adjusted ACT intervention group (ACT-Adjust) or a befriending control group, with a PMA activity present in each session. Both groups received eight sessions, for one and a half hours weekly. Measures of psychological distress significantly reduced in the ACT group compared with the befriending group. In addition, Sander *et al.* (2021) found that an eight-week ACT intervention with appropriate adaptations for 93 people with a mild to severe TBI and normal to mild memory impairment (where a PMA activity was present in seven of the sessions) significantly reduced psychological distress and also improved psychological flexibility, compared with a randomised control group.

There are currently several innovative and exciting new studies underway exploring the use of ACT in different neurological populations. The Wellbeing after Stroke (WAterS) feasibility study has investigated a nine-week online group intervention for stroke survivors. The approach is informed by ACT and aims to offer psychological and emotional support, with mindfulness exercises included in each session. The easy access report is available (Patchwood & Foote, 2023). Further, Dana Wong and Nick Sathananthan's research group in Australia is conducting a clinical trial of a Valued Living After Neurological Trauma (VaLiANT) eight-week ACT group programme, for adults who have suffered a stroke or acquired brain injury, which they talk about in Chapter 6 of this book, and have so far published a single-case design study in advance of the awaited trial results (Sathananthan *et al.*, 2020). Similarly, Rauwenhoff *et al.* (2023) are trialling an individual eight-week intervention of ACT in ABI (BrainACT) for feasibility and effectiveness. Also discussed later in this book, Gould *et al.* (2022) are undertaking a randomised controlled trial exploring the use of ACT adapted for people with motor neurone disease, in addition to the usual care they would receive, and compared to receiving usual care only. The study protocol is available and will be known as the COMMEND trial (Gould *et al.*, 2022). In preparing this chapter, we reached out to a number of the lead researchers, who confirmed that PMA is a key feature of their interventions, often a component of every single group or individual session, unlike other parts of the hexaflex which usually feature in one or two sessions apiece. These authors helpfully provided input into the adaptations they found useful, which have been incorporated into Table 4.1 below.

Assessment and introducing PMA

PMA may not be for everyone, and assessment for suitability is important. First, a basic level of understanding to consent to the intervention is required, as is selling the idea of PMA if there is any reticence/scepticism ('Shall we just have a brief try and see how it goes?'). If a client with a neurological condition has symptoms which could affect engagement in, and repeated practice of, PMA (e.g. receptive language difficulties, distractibility, memory issues), then rather than discount this intervention, we would advocate modifying it (e.g. using shorter scripts, recording sessions). Our ideas for modification are outlined in Table 4.1. Or, if PMA does not feel acceptable or manageable to the client, you could start working on the other aspects of the hexaflex and maybe return to PMA once a framework of acceptance and commitment has been cultivated within the therapeutic relationship.

Regarding potential contraindications and preventing adverse events, Wong *et al.*'s (2018) systematic review of randomised controlled trials of mindfulness-based therapies indicate very few adverse events linked to mindfulness-based interventions. However, they suggest that attention should be paid to temporary negative emotions and increased depression and anxiety, and muscle soreness during practice. The authors further point out that many of the research studies screened for conditions such as post-traumatic stress disorder (PTSD), psychosis and suicidality, which should be carefully considered and assessed in clinical practice with people who have neurological conditions to ensure appropriate treatment is being provided. There has also been some recent research to indicate increases in false memory acquisition following mindfulness practice (e.g. Ayache *et al.*, 2022; Bitton, Chatburn & Immink, 2023; Sherman & Grange, 2020), which may particularly affect our clients with significant memory impairments and/or those with a tendency to become fixed on particular beliefs or standpoints. However, this research is in its infancy and any impact in real-world terms remains unclear. Given the research to date, significant difficulties are highly unlikely to be encountered when employing the low intensity PMA strategies offered in this chapter.

CLINICAL CASE STUDY

A client Natalie Hampson has recently been working with is also a good example of the benefits of increasing PMA for someone with a severe brain injury.

NB (pseudonym chosen by client) was a keen cyclist and belonged to an amateur cycling club. During an organised ride he suffered life-changing physical and cognitive injuries following a collision. Five years on from his injury, NB continues to struggle with emotional and behavioural control, and with awareness of his cognitive difficulties, which has had a significant detrimental impact on his relationships with others. When calm, NB has described that his 'thoughts can get stuck' and he 'can't let stuff go'. He gets 'frustrated' about issues and can contact those around him many times a day in an attempt to get those problems sorted.

Through individual therapy and working closely with his support workers, NB has been able to learn a mindful breathing exercise in which he visualises his thoughts floating on waves moving out to sea. An app was trialled to help promote regular practice (*Smiling Mind* – see resources section), but NB struggled to engage with this independently. However, with prompts from support workers, he has been able to engage in mindfulness practice on a regular basis and also to implement this strategy at times of heightened distress, which has allowed him to unhook from his thoughts and reduce his physical stress levels. In turn, this has allowed him to respond more appropriately to others and make more rational and informed plans to solve problems by reasoning more effectively about the issues at hand.

For example, NB's wheelchair recently slid down a steep slope. He was understandably very distressed by this and became fixed in his thinking about throwing the wheelchair away and wanting to start ringing his case manager. He rated himself as 100/100 on his 'frustration' thermometer (0 = no problems, 100 = worst ever). After scaffolded conversation to help him think through the issue, he still rated himself as 50/100 and agreed to engage in his mindfulness exercise, which was brief (three to four minutes). After successfully bringing his focus back to the present moment, he reported his stress levels had dropped to 10/100 and he spontaneously reasoned, 'I'll just not use that wheelchair for that [journey] again.'

Patient feedback on present moment awareness in stroke

We thought it would be beneficial to include a couple of quotes about what consumers of PMA within research studies had to say about their experience of it. This client feedback was gathered by Patchwood and Foote (2023) following their WAterS intervention (currently in preparation for publication) and helpfully shared with us for this chapter. We thought these artfully captured the essence of PMA from a 'customer' perspective of someone with an ABI:

> The main thing is the mindfulness ... at the time when I was doing it, it was, I have to say I thought it was a little bit, almost like self-centred, it made me feel like I'm concentrating on me, but actually in the couple of months since the study, I understand the benefit of it, and it's a great help. The actual mindfulness has helped with regards to those particular days where I'm ... over-loaded with information, the mindfulness helps me re-focus. (WAterS research participant)

> Mindfulness is different, because you can do it with your eyes open, you can do it with your eyes closed ... there's no correct way in how to do it, there's no correct scenario ... you don't have to dress in particular clothing or anything, you can do it wherever and whenever, and it's just a case of touching base, really, with every aspect. (WAterS research participant)

Adaptations to present moment awareness interventions for people with ABI

As a result of an individual's unique array of difficulties following an ABI, adapted PMA practice/exercises must be tailored to the person, rather than to a diagnosis per se, as neurological presentations are highly heterogeneous. That said, here are some general ideas for adapting PMA for people with physical and cognitive difficulties secondary to ABI.

Table 4.1: Adapting PMA for people with physical and cognitive difficulties following ABI

PMA technique	Suggested adaptations	
	Cognitive difficulty	Physical difficulty
Explaining PMA	Break information down into smaller chunks, work at a slower pace, and repeat information.	Use pictures and/or tactile or auditory materials to account for sensory difficulties, explain and help to consolidate metaphors (see resources section).
	Use simplified, less abstract metaphors incorporating previously established knowledge (e.g. the use of an anchor on a boat, leaves on a stream, clouds in the sky).	Prioritise quality of access to PMA experiences in sessions, over rigid adherence to the treatment manual.
	Break down larger metaphors into sub-metaphors, revisiting them over several sessions, adding more to consolidate learning, recall and meaning.	Focus on visualisation or exteroception rather than body/breathing if the client has a physical deficit, and vice versa if a visual deficit.
	Use Russ Harris's YouTube videos for brief, enjoyable introductions to ACT concepts – see resources section.	Some of the 'struggle' that people experience during mindfulness activities can be useful for post-activity discussion points and presents an opportunity to emphasise the 'sitting with suffering' perspective of ACT.
	Geoff Hill (2020) suggests being bold with metaphors, even if you're not sure the client will be able to work with it straight away, and if cognitive difficulties arise, offering support to turn towards the discomfort, exploring, allowing and making room for it.	Experiment with modelling the noticing of your own thoughts out loud during the process (Hill, 2020). For example, 'I'm having the thought that I'm not sure how this metaphor/explanation is going, and if you're thinking I can't understand the physical difficulties you have, but I wonder, if you're willing, we can try together?'

PMA technique	Suggested adaptations	
	Cognitive difficulty	Physical difficulty
Dropping anchor and brief PMA exercises	Use a consistent cue to start the practice to help transition more quickly into PMA. Identify interoceptive and/or exteroceptive anchors the individual prefers. Use frequent repetition for consolidation – homework tasks using memory aids. Use of the same ideas, visual cues, metaphors – establish what they prefer and reinforce throughout multiple practices. Have a cue card for pocket, for example STOP, DROP ANCHOR, FOCUS ON X. Do noticing five things exercise (of each: see, hear and feel somewhere on your skin). It's quick, multi-modal, easy to adapt (leaving out any modality/just using one) and helps to practise focused attention. Our clients like its simplicity and that you can do it in different places to notice different things. Minimise focus on time and length of breathing if there is a need to reduce cognitive demand, for example prioritise slowed breathing and longer outbreath rather than counting the length of breath or specifying number of seconds of each breath. However, if part of the purpose is to greater engage attentional processing, then demands can be increased, for example breathe in for four seconds and out for six seconds.	Consider physical difficulties and/or pain with moving or sensing parts of the body, hypersensitivity; consider consulting with physiotherapy. Alternative grounding anchors: • Breath. • Feet on floor. • Contact between the body and chair. • Any body part that can feel contact with something external. • Clothes on any part of skin that feels comfortable. • Use of a bracelet or watch to touch. • An externally focused anchor, such as a scan of what they are wearing, or a chosen item in the environment. • Use of whatever senses are available to the person for the 'Five senses' exercise. Two senses of scanning outward for what you can see and hear works well. Track thoughts in time exercise with the eyes/in the mind rather than tracking with the finger. See resources section for free online YouTube PMA videos to use.

Mindful guided practice	Keep it brief – see resources section for brief STOP scripts.	ABI may result in visual neglect or physical impairment or weakness, which could make it difficult for someone to pay attention to their environment or bodily sensations on one or both sides of the body. It is important to establish what the person is comfortable with and what would be beneficial to work through.
	Take regular breaks if needed.	
	Use Niels Detert's YouTube video to help maintain attentional focus (see resources section).	
	Use written calendar/diarised/scheduled alarm prompts to promote regular practice.	Give 'warnings' about only involving as much as they are comfortable with in body scan exercises, particularly if the person has painful bodily sensations as a result of the ABI.
	Consider recording sessions for later playback to consolidate information.	
	See resources section for a mindfulness of breath exercise adapted by a speech and language therapist for people with expressive and receptive language difficulties.	Consider whether a body scan is appropriate in light of physical deficits.
		Notice minimal eye (or other body part) movement for significant physical impairment.
		People may find bringing their awareness to a paralysed limb scary or uncomfortable. However, drawing attention to it may increase awareness and/or acceptance, depending on the goal.
		Tinnitus is a common physical consequence of ABI that may be exacerbated by mindfulness. However, using mindfulness as a way to specifically aid in managing physical difficulties can be beneficial, for example through observing the tinnitus noise in a more accepting and non-judgemental way. An exteroceptive PMA exercise may also be useful instead.
		Set realistic mindfulness practice targets in light of fatigue/support needs/rehab programmes and so on. Invite a commitment to practise, no matter how small.

PMA technique	Suggested adaptations	
	Cognitive difficulty	Physical difficulty
Extero-ceptive exercises	Encourage looking, where able, towards different parts of the environment and moving to direct attentional focus towards them. Try forest bathing exercises and use of mindful movement – see Delaney and MacDonald (2023)/resources. Collect items when in nature, and touch to cue into exercises when back at home.	Adapted exercise (see resources). Mindful listening to music. Use an ice-cube or drink if there are swallowing difficulties (if manageable for the person); consider consulting with speech and language therapy. Use an object (touching or looking at). Forest bathing with a plant at home (e.g. Song *et al.* (2017), with red roses).

Resources for PMA for people with ABI and other neurological conditions

This section includes the following resources:

- Mindfulness STOP script (from VaLiANT trial) – see appendix below.
- Brief 'Five things' exercise – see appendix.

We also recommend:

- Russ Harris YouTube channel – very accessible and short animations for people with ABI explaining ACT metaphors and techniques – www.youtube.com/@dr.russharris-acceptanceco972

- Mindfulness training after brain injury with Dr Niels Detert (20 minutes and 40 seconds) – www.youtube.com/watch?v=H-h1yqOlr70E (excellent introduction to mindfulness).

- Mindfulness of breath exercise, adapted for people with expressive and receptive language difficulties, written by Natalie Hampson and Clare Barr (specialist neuro speech and language therapist).

- WAterS trial YouTube exercises – https://bit.ly/WATERSvideos [bit.ly]. Two videos on guided noticing of the breath (five minutes, five seconds) and guided noticing of the body practice (15 minutes, 59 seconds) designed for stroke survivors.

- Delaney and MacDonald's Neuro in Nature website – www.neuroinnature.co.uk (offering forest bathing information and guided sessions in the UK (North-West currently)).

- *Smiling Mind* app: a free mindfulness app with a wide range of different types and length of exercises – www.smilingmind.com.au/smiling-mind-app

- Mindfulness exercises aimed at stroke survivors, including brief breathing, physical senses, body scan and mindful movement exercises (less than five minutes each) (whole video: 25 minutes and 29 seconds) – www.youtube.com/watch?v=tPvwzPBGGo8

Summary

We hope that our chapter will help you to incorporate PMA into your clinical practice with people with ABI with confidence in its effectiveness, and some helpful resources. We very much enjoy this work and seeing its benefits in our clients and have welcomed the opportunity to share our thoughts and experiences.

References

Ayache, J., Abichou, K., La Corte, V., Piolino, P. & Sperduti, M. (2022). Mindfulness and false memories: State and dispositional mindfulness does not increase false memories for naturalistic scenes presented in a virtual environment. *Psychology Research and Behavior Management*, 86(2), 571–584. doi: 10.1007/s00426-021-01504-7

Bitton, S., Chatburn, A. & Immink, M. A. (2023). The influence of focused attention and open monitoring mindfulness meditation states on true and false memory. *Journal of Cognitive Enhancement*, 30, 1–16. doi: 10.1007/s41465-023-00259-w

Curvis, W. & Methley, A. (eds). (2021). *Acceptance and Commitment Therapy and Brain Injury: A Practical Guide for Clinicians*. London: Routledge.

Delaney, M. & McDonald, C. (2023). Neuro in Nature. www.neuroinnature.co.uk

Detert, N. B. (2015). Mindfulness for neurologists. *Practical Neurology*, 15(5), 369–374.

Gould, R. L., Thompson, B. J., Rawlinson, C., Kumar, P. *et al.* (2022). A randomised controlled trial of Acceptance and Commitment Therapy plus usual care compared to usual care alone for improving psychological health in people with motor neuron disease (COMMEND): Study protocol. *BMC Neurology,* 22, 431. doi: 10.1186/s12883-022-02950-5

Gregg, J. A., Callaghan, G. M., Hayes, S. C. & Glenn-Lawson, J. L. (2007). Improving diabetes self-management through acceptance, mindfulness, and values: A randomized controlled trial. *Journal of Consulting and Clinical Psychology,* 75(2), 336–343.

Harris, R. (2019). *ACT Made Simple: An Easy-to-Read Primer on Acceptance and Commitment Therapy.* Oakland, CA: New Harbinger Publications.

Hayes, S. C., Strosahl, K. D. & Wilson, K. G. (2012). *Acceptance and Commitment Therapy: The Process and Practice of Mindful Change* (second edition). New York, NY: Guilford Press.

Hill, G. (2020). Challenges and opportunities in ACT and neurological conditions: The Dysexecuflex. South Tees Hospitals NHS Foundation Trust/British Psychological Society. (Available from the author via Researchgate.net.)

Hill, G., Hynd, N., Price, J., Evans, S., Moffitt, J. & Brechin, D. (2017). Living Well with Neurological Conditions: An eight-week series of group workshops informed by Acceptance and Commitment Therapy (ACT). South Tees Hospitals NHS Foundation Trust. (Available from the author via Researchgate.net.)

Jani, B. D., Simpson, R., Lawrence, M., Simpson, S. & Mercer, S. W. (2018). Acceptability of mindfulness from the perspective of stroke survivors and caregivers: A qualitative study. *Pilot and Feasibility Studies,* 4(1), Article 57. https://doi.org/10.1186/s40814-018-0244-1

Kabat-Zinn, J. (2003). Mindfulness-based stress reduction (MBSR). *Constructivism in the Human Sciences,* 8(2), 73–107.

Kangas, M. & McDonald, S. (2011). Is it time to act? The potential of acceptance and commitment therapy for psychological problems following acquired brain injury. *Neuropsychological Rehabilitation,* 21(2), 250–276.

Kashdan, T. B. & Rottenberg, J. (2010). Psychological flexibility as a fundamental aspect of health. *Clinical Psychology Review,* 30(7), 865–878.

King, M. (2021). Acceptance and Commitment Therapy for People Experiencing Seizures. In W. Curvis & A. Methley (eds), *Acceptance and Commitment Therapy and Brain Injury: A Practical Guide for Clinicians* (pp.79–91). London: Routledge.

Kotera, Y., Richardson, M. & Sheffield, D. (2022). Effects of shinrin-yoku (forest bathing) and nature therapy on mental health: A systematic review and meta-analysis. *International Journal of Mental Health and Addiction,* 20, 337–361. doi: 10.1007/s11469-020-00363-4

Lovette, B. C., Kanaya, M. R., Bannon, S. M., Vranceanu, A-M. & Greenberg, J. (2022). Hidden gains? Measuring the impact of mindfulness-based interventions for people with mild traumatic brain injury: A scoping review. *Brain Injury,* 36(9), 1059–1070. doi: 10.1080/02699052.2022.2109745

Mak, T. C. T., Wong, T. W. L. & Ng, S. M. S. (2023). The use of mindfulness-based interventions in stroke rehabilitation: A scoping review. *Rehabilitation Psychology,* 68(3), 221–234. doi: 10.1037/rep0000505

McEwan, K., Krogh, K. S., Dunlop, K., Khan, M. & Krogh, A. (2023). Virtual forest bathing programming as experienced by disabled adults with mobility impairments and/or low energy: A qualitative study. *Forests,* 14(5), 1033.

Niraj, S., Wright, S. & Powell, S. (2020). A qualitative study exploring the experiences of mindfulness training in people with acquired brain injury. *Neuropsychological Rehabilitation*, 30(4), 731–752. doi: 10.1080/09602011.2018.1515086

Patchwood, E. & Foote, H. (2023). *Wellbeing After Stroke (WAterS): Report on research study findings.* Available at: https://bit.ly/watersreport

Rabinowitz, A. R. & Levin, H. S. (2014). Cognitive sequelae of traumatic brain injury. *Psychiatric Clinics*, 37(1), 1–11.

Rauwenhoff, J. C., Bol, Y., van Heugten, C. M., Batink, T. *et al.* (2023). Acceptance and commitment therapy for people with acquired brain injury: Rationale and description of the BrainACT treatment. *Clinical Rehabilitation*, 37(8), 1011–1025. doi: 10.1177/02692155231154124

Sander, A. M., Clark, A. N., Arciniegas, D. B., Tran, K., *et al.* (2021). A randomized controlled trial of acceptance and commitment therapy for psychological distress among persons with traumatic brain injury. *Neuropsychological Rehabilitation*, 31(7), 1105–1129. doi: 10.1080/09602011.2020.1762670

Sathananthan, N., Dimech-Betancourt, B., Morris, E., Vicendese, D. *et al.* (2020). A single-case experimental evaluation of a new group-based intervention to enhance adjustment to life with acquired brain injury: VaLiANT (Valued Living After Neurological Trauma). *Neuropsychological Rehabilitation*, 32(8), 2170–2202. doi: 10.1080/09602011.2021.1971094

Sherman, S. M. & Grange, J. A. (2020). Exploring the impact of mindfulness on false-memory susceptibility. *Psychological Science*, 31(8), 968–977. doi: 10.1177/0956797620929302

Smart, E., Curvis, W. & Methley, A. (2021). Integrating Acceptance and Commitment Therapy Principles in Acute Care Settings. In W. Curvis & A. Methley (eds), *Acceptance and Commitment Therapy and Brain Injury: A Practical Guide for Clinicians* (pp.150–164). London: Routledge.

Song, C., Igarashi, M., Ikei, H. & Miyazaki, Y. (2017). Physiological effects of viewing fresh red roses. *Complementary Therapy Medicine*, 35, 78–84.

Wang, X., Thiel, L. & de Graff, N. (2022). Mindfulness and relaxation techniques for stroke survivors with aphasia: A feasibility and acceptance study. *Healthcare (Basel)*, 10(8), 1409. doi: 10.3390/healthcare10081409

Whiting, D. L., Deane, F., McLeod, H., Ciarrochi, J. & Simpson, G. (2020). Can acceptance and commitment therapy facilitate psychological adjustment after a severe traumatic brain injury? A pilot randomized controlled trial. *Neuropsychological Rehabilitation*, 30(7), 1348–1371. doi: 10.1080/09602011.2019.1583582

Wong, S. Y. S., Chan, J. Y. C., Zhang, D., Lee, E. K. P. & Tsoi, K. K. F. (2018). The safety of mindfulness-based interventions: A systematic review of randomized controlled trials. *Mindfulness*, 9, 1344–1357. doi: 10.1007/s12671-018-0897-0

Wrapson, W., Dorrestein, M., Wrapson, J., Theadom, A. *et al.* (2021). A feasibility study of a one-to-one mindfulness-based intervention for improving mood in stroke survivors. *Mindfulness*, 12(5), 1148–1158. doi: 10.1007/s12671-020-01583-4

Yi, Y., Seo, E. & An, J. (2022). Does forest therapy have physio-psychological benefits? A systematic review and meta-analysis of randomized controlled trials. *International Journal of Environmental Research and Public Health*, 19(17), 1051–1052.

Appendix – resources
Mindfulness exercise – STOP

(Included with kind permission from Dana Wong; material from the VaLiANT trial, in which this exercise is presented three times across the intervention, with a recording provided to participants for home practice.)

S = Stop

Sit up in your chair. We are going to try and stay alert and aware during this exercise. I suggest that you close your eyes; however, if you don't wish to do that, you could find a spot just in front of you to focus your eyes. Push your feet firmly into floor and feel ground beneath you.

T = Take a breath

Take a few deep breaths. Follow the air as it comes in through your nostrils and goes down to the bottom of your lungs. Then follow it as it goes back out again. Notice the air moving in and out of your nostrils. Notice the gentle rise and fall of your ribcage, and of your tummy. Put your hand on your ribcage or your tummy and feel it rising and falling as you take each breath.

You might find your mind trying to take your attention away from your breath. It might be noticing some noise in the background, or it might be telling you that this is boring, or that it's hard, or some other judgement. When it does this, just notice what your mind is doing or saying, and then gently bring your attention back to your breath. Observe the sensations in your nose, mouth, ribcage and tummy when you breathe in and out.

O = Observe

Whatever feelings, urges or sensations arise, whether pleasant or unpleasant, gently acknowledge them, as if nodding your head at people passing by you on the street. Gently acknowledge their presence, and let them be. Allow them to come and go as they please, and keep your attention on the breath. If you have any discomfort, like itching, tightness, pain or restlessness, see whether you can resist the urge to change or alter it. Just let it be there, and be gentle with it, like you might carry a puppy in distress.

P = Proceed

Bring your attention to why you're here today. Try to push beyond the reasons that are on the surface, like maybe your therapist or family member said you should come. Why are you REALLY here? What is it that matters to you about making your life more satisfying and meaningful? How do you want to be as a person, a son or daughter, a sister or brother, a partner, a friend and as a member of this group? Take a moment to acknowledge what you had to do to be here today. You needed to arrange transport, make plans to be here on time, deal with the stress of finding the place you needed to go, perhaps ask favours of other people, and work through the worries you might have about meeting new people in this group. Now that you are here, how do you want to be as a learner, as a group participant, as a human being, in order to experience a sense of purpose and contentment?

Now, with this sense of awareness of yourself, being open to everything you notice, and having a sense of your purpose, bring your attention back to the room here and now. When you are ready, bring yourself back to the room and open your eyes.

STOP exercise for language problems

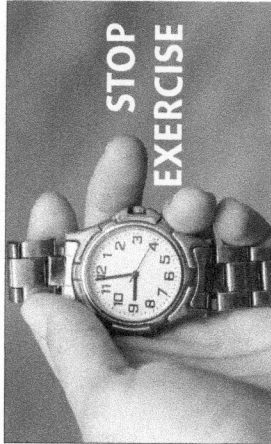

STOP EXERCISE

S = STOP

- Drop anchor

- Sit

- Close your eyes

T = TAKE A DEEP BREATH

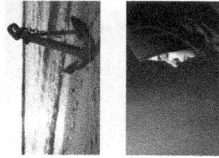

- Deep breaths
- In...out...
- Hand on tummy...
  in...out

O = OBSERVE

- Thoughts will come
  into your mind –
  that's normal.
- Let them float by,
  like leaves on a stream
- Focus on your breath,
  in...out...

P = PROCEED

- Open your eyes
- Continue with
  your day

Brief 'Five things' exercise

Take a moment to quietly notice what you are experiencing right now.

First, notice and name five things that you can see – maybe things you have not noticed before, a cobweb, a shadow, a stain on the floor.

Second, notice and name five things you can hear – even if it's very quiet, what can you get? You can usually always hear your breath even if there are not many other sounds around.

And third, notice and name five things you can feel on your skin. It could be the pressure of the chair under your bottom, the feel of your sleeve on your wrist or collar/your hair touching your neck.

And, as you become more aware of your experience right now, reflect that all the things you have just noticed were all there before, all part of what it is to be you, alive right now, yet we tend not to notice them as we focus on our minds/jobs to do. Enjoy the moment of being fully present in your life, before you go back to your day.

NB – this example is provided for professionals to adapt in any way they think would be beneficial to their clients, for example reducing the number of things to identify (notice two things you can see, hear and feel), reduce the words used (maybe by cutting out the examples), or adding in a different sense (what's going on inside, beneath your skin/your internal experience/smell) or taking one out if difficult for your client to access.

CHAPTER 5

Self-as-context and Acquired Brain Injury

JAMES BRIGGS

Introduction to me and why I am interested in ACT

This chapter explores the concept of 'self-as-context', and how it can be used in work with people with neurological conditions (PwNC). I work as a clinical neuropsychologist as part of an inpatient neuro-rehabilitation multidisciplinary team. I have previously worked in outpatient and community services for ABI patients with a range of neurological conditions and worked closely with charities and third-sector organisations in the UK who support ABI patients and their families. A common theme of work across these areas has been with changes in the idea of the self, including identity, roles, sense of self, or self-awareness following ABI (Ownsworth *et al.*, 2014).

My doctoral (PhD and DClin) thesis similarly incorporated looking at conceptualisations of the 'self' using different methods, including Foucauldian discourse analysis (FDA). This analysis focuses on how language constructions make available a 'self', ways of seeing the world, and ways of being in the world (Willig, 2012). It is another way of conceptualising how language can mediate human emotions and responses, similar to relational frame theory.

For me, self-as-context has been a powerful concept when working with people to create space and perspective to talk about 'the self' more flexibly, but it is not always easy. It can be difficult to know when to introduce the concept of self-as-context, how to describe it and even whether it is necessary to discuss for some people to benefit from ACT interventions. In ABI populations, these discussions can also be further complicated by psychological and cognitive flexibility.

Introduction to chapter

This chapter does not claim to offer definitive answers on theory or *best* practice, but instead aims to note what can be helpful to explore when thinking about self-as-context in ABI populations. I aim to cover guidance that has helped me in understanding and using the concept and offer some practical exercises that can be useful in working with self-as-context.

This chapter is aimed at people working with ACT in ABI populations. It covers an introduction to the concept of self-as-context, and suggestions on how to introduce the concept with people we work with. I then talk a little about how it may relate to other issues important in ABI work, including cognitive flexibility, denial and wider systems around the person. The aim of this is to help formulate and think about adaptations which could be useful. It finishes with an example of this work. It is hoped the reader will come away feeling more confident to discuss self-as-context and incorporate it into sessions.

Self-as-context

Although there are a vast number of ways we can talk about 'self', ACT traditionally focuses on three senses of self. These are self-concept, or 'conceptualised self' (i.e. who I am as a person, how I depict myself); self-as-awareness (i.e. a process of noticing our experiences); and self-as-context (Harris, 2009).

Self-as-context is a viewpoint from which we can observe thoughts and feelings, and a space in which those thoughts and feelings can move. It is therefore often referred to as the 'observing self'. From this viewpoint, we can separate from, observe and transcend all our thoughts, emotions, values, judgements and memories. This can be accessed by 'noticing what we are noticing' or becoming conscious of our own consciousness. Self-as-context is a key skill in the ACT hexaflex, related to increasing awareness. It is also inherent in other ACT treatment components, particularly defusion (Chapter 3) and contact with the present moment (Chapter 4), and provides a stable perspective from which to be psychologically flexible (Godbee & Kangas, 2020). Self-as-context has been theorised to be important in enabling or facilitating several related experiences, including theory of mind, empathy, compassion and acceptance (Harris, 2009).

It is easy to get caught up in terminology and philosophical conceptualisations of the self here. Self-as-context 'is an experience beyond all words...as it has no physical properties' (Harris, 2009, p.175). Trying to introduce an experience beyond all words is obviously difficult and can lead to avoidance by clinicians (Westrup, 2014). However, when introduced well, at a point that can be understood and importantly practised, this concept can be powerful. If we can observe thoughts, feelings and roles as dynamic, and acknowledge they are influenced by context, we are less likely to become fused with them and led in unhelpful directions.

What does self-as-context look like?

Inability to connect with self-as-context, or an observing self, maintains a rigid sense-of-self, or 'conceptualised-self'. This might include inflexible self-statements, such as 'I am a good person', 'I am a hard worker', 'I am a runner', 'I am a teacher'. People with an inflexible conceptualised self will likely experience 'stuckness' with perspective taking, empathy and compassion for self, and struggle with openness to differing points of view. This may include working hard to maintain a sense of self-consistency and distortion or re-interpretation of events and situations to maintain a clear self-concept.

Contrastingly, people able to access self-as-context can utilise the 'observing self' and observe psychological and physical experiences from a different transcendental perspective. This can be experienced as noticing that you are noticing, or awareness of being aware. Self-as-context offers the opportunity for flexible perspective taking (e.g. 'I hold multiple roles', 'There are lots of different parts to me').

The importance of self-as-context for people with neurological conditions

Following ABI, many people can experience a rapid and immense shift in their thoughts and feelings about life, abilities and roles. Often the system around them can emphasise how ABI has led to changes to a conceptualised self. This can lead to framing of an incongruence with post-ABI self-concept, and pre-injury or anticipated future selves. People may describe themselves in relation to qualities which no longer appear viable and/or accessible due to their ABI, including previous roles, mobility, cognitive capabilities and responsibilities.

Discrepancy between one's pre-injury and post-injury self-concept has long been proposed to mediate anxiety and depression, and influence engagement and progress in rehabilitation (Gracey, Evans & Malley, 2009). Heightened distress associated with persisting negative self-discrepancies can produce a sense of hopelessness and lead to maladaptive coping. Drawing on self-as-context can offer another perspective away from conflict and discrepancy. It is important that any challenge or questioning of rigid self-concepts should be done in an empathetic and validating manner (Cameron, Oliver & Curvis, 2021). Any conversation about the self or identity is likely to bring up frames of reference to roles at work, family and ability, which could trigger distress. However, supportively helping people to become aware of and release some of their hold on these identities and roles can help offer alternative perspectives and facilitate value-based action.

Little research has been conducted which explicitly looks at the effectiveness of self-as-context work in ABI. This is perhaps for the reasons outlined above including the difficulty conceptualising and measuring self-as-context, as well as the difficulty in disentangling it from other skills and psychological processes. However, self-as-context is compatible with the aims of holistic neuro-rehabilitation (Kangas & McDonald, 2011) and specific targets of ABI work, outlined below.

Can ABI limit self-as-context work?

The observing self's ability to take perspective is potentially impacted by structural damage and cognitive impairment. This is touched on below and discussed in greater detail by Whiting and colleagues (2017).

Anecdotally, in speaking with friends, colleagues and experts who use ACT (or even developed the model), there is little clear consensus on whether cognitive ability is necessary to support the observing self. I have spoken with professionals who view brain injury as deleterious to self-as-context. Some even purposely avoid discussing self-as-context in people where there are marked cognitive impairments or concerns around 'insight' or self-awareness. However, research has supported ACT as beneficial for people with severe brain injury, suggesting that cognitive impairment and self-awareness changes do not negate this work (Whiting *et al.*, 2012). Rather, it appears important to be patient-centred in adjusting language, information and experiential work with the individual with cognitive impairment. Conceptualising an observing self, as an awareness skill that is always there, can be helpful to discuss early and often.

It can be helpful when introducing self-as-context to differentiate the observing self from a 'mind' organised by the physical brain. Damage to the physical brain can lead to impairment in cognitive skills. However, ACT conceptualises the mind, self-concept and capability in terms of linguistic relational frames, and so this causal link is not as certain. Self-as-context fosters a sense of self, separate to the physical brain. It should therefore follow that changes to the physical self should not limit self-as-context, but it may require thought and adaptation to help people to access it following ABI.

Metacognition is self-regulated insight into one's own thinking (Toglia & Kirk, 2000) and is perhaps conceptually the closest cognitive skill to self-as-context. Metacognitive skills can change following brain injury, and metacognitive rehabilitation is useful in supporting self-awareness (INCOG, 2024). However, theoretically, self-as-context seems more than just this cognitive skill (Harris, 2019). Improving metacognition through metacognitive training could feasibly improve someone's ability to distinguish their thoughts as they arise, and ability to engage in experiential work. I am not aware of any studies that have investigated this link between metacognition and self-as-context awareness practice, but it would be an interesting area to explore.

Self-awareness and self-as-context

Self-awareness can be distinguished from self-conceptualisation, as the accuracy of self-appraisal. Many ABI populations experience changes in self-awareness, or 'insight', regarding their functional limitations (Robertson & Schmitter-Edgecombe, 2015). Although the literature is replete with information about self-awareness difficulties, there is no universally accepted definition. One commonly accepted interpretation in the rehabilitation literature defines self-awareness using two similar constructs: a) possessing an objective knowledge regarding the existence of one's deficits and b) possessing a subjective understanding of the significance of those deficits to functional performance (Mamman, 2022; Toglia & Kirk, 2000).

Self-awareness has been divided into three interdependent awareness levels: intellectual, emergent and anticipatory awareness (Crosson *et al.*, 1989; Toglia & Maeir, 2018). Intellectual awareness is considered the 'lowest' awareness level and is defined as a person's basic understanding of the existence of a deficit (Toglia & Maeir, 2018). At this level, people can comprehend that one or more specific functional skills are impaired (Chesnel *et al.*, 2018). Emergent awareness refers to an ability to recognise and self-monitor difficulties as they occur. Anticipatory awareness is the most refined level of awareness and involves the ability to anticipate that some difficulties will be experienced in future situations, because of deficits secondary to ABI (Chesnel *et al.*, 2018).

Decreased self-awareness on any of these levels has been shown to translate into poor judgement and poor safety (Skidmore *et al.*, 2018), dysfunctional interpersonal relationships (Bivona *et al.*, 2015; Chesnel *et al.*, 2018), the inability to set realistic goals (Fleming, Strong & Ashton, 1996), and poor compliance with and participation in rehabilitation (Geytenbeek *et al.*, 2017).

There can be a pull towards clinicians emphasising difficulties and impairment in these situations, often to emphasise safety and minimise potential risk (e.g. 'Remember, you can't walk without help'). However, this emphasises frames around unhelpful comparison, discrepancy and distress (e.g. 'I can't walk anymore'). While it is important to ensure patient safety, it is also important to explore and formulate these as problematic thoughts, feelings and behaviours rather than an 'impaired' problematic self (e.g. 'I notice I can get a strong urge to try and walk without help, and notice feelings of frustration and sadness when people tell me not to; and notice I feel angry when I disagree with people about what might happen if I try'). Raising awareness of those cognitive difficulties, behaviours or functional skill deficits which could cause problems from an observing self-perspective can help reduce associated distress. Writing these down and making them tangible for the individual can be extremely informative and helpful for them and their family.

I have occasionally used the three levels of self-awareness to ask people what they notice they are able to observe at different levels. For example, I ask them to 'notice that they are noticing' when discussing any impairment, experiencing in-the-moment challenges, or thinking about how ABI-related changes may impact them in future situations. Asking circular questions around what their family and/or therapy team may notice, think or feel can also facilitate this change in perspective and connection with self-as-context.

Denial

Sudden and traumatic changes to conceptualised selves can trigger emotional defences such as denial. Some people will attempt to protect, retain or 'shield conceptualisation of the self even when it leads to ineffective action, to attempt to protect the individual from experiencing anxiety' (Prigatano, 2012, p.374). The anxiety can be seen as related to the discontinuity of a clear self-concept following ABI (Cantor et al., 2005; Prigatano & Sherer, 2020). Denial can therefore be triggered when confronted by discussions around changes in abilities, roles or identity. Qualitative work has highlighted that conflict between accepting 'new selves' while still desiring to return to the 'old self' tends to lead to avoidant behaviours which interfere with recovery (O'Callaghan, Powell & Oyebode, 2006). Confronting clients with clear evidence of their impairments or the need to change may well result in an increase in threat-related reactions, such as denial and avoidance (Prigatano, 1999). This is in line with other theory and practice, such as motivational interviewing (Miller & Rollnick, 2012).

Prigatano and Sherer (2020) summarise over 20 years' work with denial of disability and suggest different approaches to working in this area. For example, they suggest it can be beneficial to engage the patient in a discussion about sense of self at different points, including reflecting on sense of self prior to brain injury, and to identify challenges or negativity, talk about recent experiences they have found positive/encouraging and negative/threatening, increase their perceived sense of ability to manage negative emotions when they arise to promote a sense of hope and resiliency, and ask the patient to describe strengths and weaknesses without associating them with TBI. Directly challenging or confronting the individual with tasks they are struggling with should be avoided. As always, it is important that this work is approached with a supportive relationship that encompasses the qualities of warmth, acceptance and a non-judgemental stance (Schöenberger, Humle & Teasdale, 2006). There are clearly parallels to self-as-context, and an early introduction to the idea of self-as-context may reduce the threat, confrontation and a subsequent triggering of denial.

Adjustment, transitions and perspectives

Summary statements around conceptualisations of self are often referred to as self-identity. Diverse standpoints on self-identity have evolved for many years within philosophy, sociology and neuroscience (Beadle *et al.*, 2016). In the psychological literature, identity is broadly defined as the collective characteristics we perceive as our own, which endure over time and are continuously under construction. Self-concept refers to the overarching thoughts and feelings a person has about him or herself. The related concept of self-esteem represents an evaluative component or judgements about one's own worth or value (Ownsworth, 2014).

Relative comparisons to previous roles, and perspectives and awareness of time (speed of recovery), are important frames of reference in self-concept and self-esteem. Indeed, in ABI literature and beyond, a vast amount is written about the importance of self-concept and psychological distress. In self-concept discrepancy theory, discrepancy between one's sense of self (i.e. who I am) and ideal self (i.e. who I want to be) has been conceptualised to underlie depression, whereas discrepancy between one's sense of self and ought self (i.e. who I should be) elicits anxiety (Higgins, Klein & Strauman, 1985).

Relative comparison is not always negative. The qualitative work of Nochi has highlighted that although ABI can catalyse a sense of loss of self-identity (Nochi, 1998), for others ABI offers renewed positive ways to view self-identity. It notes that, for some, positive self-identity is shaped 'because of' brain injury (Nochi, 2000). It also outlines narratives around growth and value-based development, including positive changes people have made following ABI, re-prioritisation of 'what matters most', or social connection.

Diane Whiting has written extensively on using ACT in traumatic brain injury populations. In the ACT Adjust programme, she includes concrete written summaries of roles and 'how we see ourselves'. This can help increase awareness around self-identity and concept in different contexts, as well as continuity of self in different contexts (self-as-context). Conversations around self may include which objective and subjective aspects of self-identity (e.g. partner, parent, caring, warm) appear consistent, fragile, strengthened or changed following ABI.

I personally use the Y-shaped model often, in combination with the idea of self-as-context, to think about navigating changes in self-identity with the people I work with (see Gracey *et al.*, 2009; Gracey, Vicentijevic & Methley, 2021). The Y-shaped model is so-called because it proposes that the process of adaptation and reintegration into society following brain injury initially involves the coming to awareness, understanding and adaptive resolution of conceptual discrepancies. This resolution is depicted in the converging lines of the 'V' at the top of the 'Y'. In the Y-shaped model, 'positive identity transition' following brain injury is proposed to entail assimilation of both continuous and changed aspects of self, and consolidating an updated identity ('the new me') through regular participation in meaningful activities. This framework depicts self-identity change as a process that occurs over time, and one that is strongly influenced by social, inter- and intra-personal context (Gracey *et al.*, 2009).

An increased capacity to be open to the perspective and the possibility of different selves, experiments that explore and 'nourish' specific identities in different contexts and opening to the emotions that arise are parallel targets of the ACT hexaflex (Gracey *et al.*, 2021). Self-as-context can complement and enhance this work, by offering a language for observing and noticing, and observing changes in thoughts, behaviours, functions and even identities.

Responses of the system

Conceptualised selves can be emphasised and maintained by the family and societal pressures. Including family members in rehabilitation work is important and can reveal a great deal about the relational frames the individual is positioned within. Sabat and Harré (1992) conceptualise aspects of self-concept in neuro-disability as subject to negotiation in interactions with others. When working with family, it is helpful to identify the content of language being used around descriptors of the individual before and after ABI.

Anxiety and distress in the family and close relationships can lead to denial, but also accentuating narratives of impairment. At times, wider systems emphasise disability and reductionist summaries of impairment. This is promoted by factors such as medico-legal claims, care needs assessment and disability allowance, where there is a need to objectively state change and impairment as consequences of ABI. The family or wider system, in an effort to support the person, may adopt a disempowering position in which the person with ABI is seen as passive, disabled and lacking adult agency (Yeates *et al.*, 2007).

Again, self-as-context offers a useful position to help discuss emotive thoughts, feelings and behaviours while avoiding global descriptions of 'self'. It can be helpful to bring thoughts and concerns to discussions with family and systems, and with warmth and acceptance be able to acknowledge new behaviours or cognitive impairments which require support, but do not represent the entirety of the individual.

Self-as-context and culture

Trying to summarise cultural perspectives on self-as-context is beyond the scope of this chapter. It is important to think about and formulate a person's cultural context in the work, and acknowledge that as well as the immediate system around the person, there are countless cultural perspectives on what constitutes self-concept and self-as-context.

Consistency and contradiction of self-identity and self-concept vary across different cultures (Choi & Choi, 2002). Taking just two simplified examples: Cartesian perspectives support a confidence in a self or 'mind', where there exists a separation between self as 'I' and object as 'other'. Self-object relationships constitute a spectrum of intersubjective, social constructionist or interactional constitutions. Zen Buddhism alternatively adopts an understanding of the self as an illusion, impossible to separate from surroundings. However, they also teach the 'middle way', whose focus is a 'meta-self' able to inquire and doubt self-certainty (see Oh, 2022).

Similarly, writers have suggested that different cultures take different positions on how they conceptualise themselves in relation to other people, on a continuum of independence to interdependence with others. This is perhaps overly simplistic, as cultures likely promote multiple variations of independence or interdependence (Vignoles *et al.*, 2016). However, it is useful to reflect on how self-concept may be linked to broader interdependence with others and complex institutions, including family, religion, sports clubs, work and social media (DeAndrea, Shaw & Levine, 2010). Aiming to keep the work patient-centred and being open to what people bring when they talk about and notice when thinking about self can help ensure the work is meaningful.

Assessment

Given the complexity of conceptualising self-as-context, it is perhaps unsurprising there has been little consensus on how it can or should be assessed and there are few formal 'measures' of self-as-context. Assessment questionnaires appear to directly question agreement with statements focusing on deictic relations (relations between the self and thoughts and emotions). For example, to what extent you agree or disagree with statements such as 'you are distinct from your thoughts' (distinction statement) or 'you are the context in which your thoughts appear' (hierarchical statement) (Foody *et al.*, 2013; Yu, McCracken & Norton, 2016).

The Self-Experiences Questionnaire (SEQ) (Yu *et al.*, 2016) was developed based on the responses of patients with chronic pain. This scale is two-dimensional, assessing 'self-as-distinction' and 'self-as-observer'. For example, 'I can actually see that I am not my thoughts' is an item loading onto self-as-distinction. 'The health, appearance, and feelings of my body change, but the sense of my self who is aware of these changes is the same', is an item which loads onto self-as-observer. The authors highlight that although having good psychometric properties, it is unclear how generalisable it is in non-pain groups.

The Self-As-Context Scale (SACS) (Zettle, 2018) was developed in college samples over a series of studies. It has been shown to have two moderately correlated sub-scales: Centering and Transcending. Centering reflects the ability to act calmly to unwanted psychological experiences, while Transcending reflects perspective-taking that characterises the observing self. An example item for Centering is: 'I am able to notice my thoughts without getting caught up in them.' An example item for Transcending is: 'Even though there have been many changes in my life, I'm aware of a part of me that has witnessed it all.'

As noted throughout this chapter, self-as-context has commonalities with several other skills and traits, including fusion, mindfulness and compassion. There are assessments for these domains, as well as self-awareness more broadly (e.g. Sutton, 2016), or for deficits in awareness following brain injury (e.g. Sansonetti *et al.*, 2022).

To my knowledge, no scales of self-as-context have been validated in brain-injured populations. It is perhaps reasonable to suggest use of the SEQ and SACS with some caution and tailored to the needs and cognitive and communication skills of the individual. As is evident from the example items above, they require good comprehension and abstraction skills, which may not be appropriate for many people following ABI (or preceding). Personally, I have found it helpful to assess more qualitatively with the individual their ability to comprehend and engage with self-as-context work through metaphor and experiential exercises.

Techniques: Ways of introducing the idea through metaphor and experiential exercises

Ways of introducing the concept of self-as-context should always be patient-centred. As with non-ABI groups, it can be helpful to use metaphor to introduce the idea, and it is good to have several to help discussion. Clinicians should also be open to people adapting these to make them accessible and personally meaningful.

It is also helpful to make these clear and concise, and acknowledge that people's ability to engage with abstraction and complex verbal information can be compromised in ABI. ABI groups may struggle to attend, recall or utilise working memory and abstract reasoning to understand and remember complex concepts and metaphor. They may therefore need support and scaffolding when introducing these metaphors, including written summaries or visual or tangible prompts. Repetition and rehearsal of the concepts is useful, and it is important to incorporate experiential exercises alongside these introductions.

Metaphors, for the most part, reference the relationship between something constant, and an associated counterpoint which is relatively transient. The constant is the observing self, the dynamic part could be the 'thinking self', or multiple other self-concepts. For the sake of brevity, I will not go into scripts here, and these metaphors are only suggestions. Please see Harris (2019) for examples of scripts. Some examples include the following, although if there is a more personally meaningful metaphor to the individual, take time to develop that together:

94

Mountain or sky, and the weather: This observing part of you is the mountain or sky, and the changing weather can be thought of as the changing roles, thoughts and behaviours. The weather changes continually, but no matter how much it changes, the mountain or sky remains constant. And no matter how bad or how good the weather can be, it will continue to change.

Table or container: This observing part of you could be thought of as the table, with different items on it, different roles, thoughts and behaviours. This can also be conceptualised as a container with objects placed inside. This can be physically brought into session, with people asked to put personally meaningful items or self-descriptions on the table. Alternatively, a person can write his or her thoughts, feelings, sensations and memories on pieces of paper and place them in a clear container that the person then holds.

> The internal experiences are separate from and smaller than the person holding the container. The person can observe the pieces of paper from any perspective and, even if the pieces were to change, the person observing them does not change. Importantly, the person can act in the service of his or her values while still holding the glass. (Godbee & Kangas, 2020, p.918)

Chessboard: The chessboard is the observing self, and the pieces give seemingly limitless combinations of thoughts and behaviours. One colour of pieces could represent positive thoughts, feelings and emotions, and the other, the negative. Rather than trying to win every game as a side, it can be easier to be the chessboard and be connected to the game, but able to distinguish from it, and provide space for the pieces to move around.

Lego: Cameron, Oliver and Curvis (2021) emphasise the importance of making metaphor validating to the individual. They describe an effective metaphor around Lego created by a patient. Although there is an initial plan or design when you buy a Lego set, there are many ways in which the pieces of Lego can combine to make different things, and not just one 'correct' way – just as there is no one correct way of being, or correct self-identity.

Superhero/Celebrity/Respected individual: This is adapted slightly from metaphoric identity mapping (Ylvisaker *et al.*, 2008). I may ask a person to think of someone they respect, and we can find multiple pictures or draw multiple pictures of them in their different roles. This might be as a sports person, family member, charity worker and so on. We can talk about how we have some sense of them, but they have multiple selves, and most often there has been some change in their roles over time. There is no one fixed self, even if this person has a strong identity and values.

Torch: Self-as-context is the locus from which a person's experience unfolds. It can be thought of as the place from which observations are made. It is like the light from a torch shining light on different things at different times. It can focus into a narrow beam or broaden into a wide angle. Self-as-context is not the object it focuses on, and similarly the objects cannot alter this beam, but may reflect the light in different ways. It is possible to bring a torch into a session to show this to people as you describe this metaphor.

With each of these metaphors it is helpful to make them tangible, to reduce the demand on cognitive skills, including abstraction, recall and comprehension. For the above metaphors this could include using pictures of personally meaningful landscapes in different weather or seasons; bringing personal objects and putting them on a table; bringing a chessboard and moving the pieces; or playing with Lego. It may be useful to draw metaphors that the person creates, or even make short videos. People can also use ideas from the metaphors as reminders or grounding exercises when they feel stuck, for example cueing people to look out of the window at the sky, or a picture of a mountain on their wall, or a few bricks of Lego in a prominent place. Lego also offers keyrings of Lego pieces (I receive no commission).

With the table metaphor, I have previously asked family members to bring in photos or personally meaningful objects from different stages in their life, preferably from as early in life to as recent as possible. This can help support people to connect with the sense of a changing physical body, priorities, skills and abilities at different stages of life, but some sense of continuity of the self. I will sometimes combine this metaphor with one about objects on a table, where we are not the photos or meaningful objects on the table, but instead are the table (or simply observing items on the table) – able to observe and hold these values and meaningful experiences (helpful and unhelpful).

This can be supported by an experiential 'add on' of a mindfulness exercise of supporting the person to notice thoughts and emotions that arise when doing this work, and raising awareness that they are noticing these emotions. 'When we talk about X, there is X [emotion/thought], and there *you* are, noticing X' (Harris, 2009).

Russ Harris outlines some of the problems that clinicians can encounter generally when introducing the idea of self-as-context (Harris, 2019). One is to quickly add it into a session, without giving a clear intention or purpose as to how it can be beneficial. Similarly, they note that making it too abstract or mythical can make it hard for people to understand. To avoid these issues, these introductions need to be tied to experiences. Using metaphor alone and neglecting experiential exercises can be too abstract. To paraphrase Confucius: if you hear you forget, if you see you remember, if you do you understand.

Experiential 'notice you are noticing' guidance is important. This can include asking the person to notice thoughts, or 'self-talk', including thoughts or feelings about the concept or metaphors immediately when they have been introduced. 'Can you notice yourself thinking of an image?'... 'Can you notice any confusion or emotions as we speak?'... 'That is the observing self, noticing and observing.'

Similarly, it can be helpful to bring in the senses and build on mindfulness exercises. If people have a favourite snack or piece of music, ask them to eat it or listen to it. Guide them to connect mindfully with their senses, and then with the idea that there is part of them (senses in the mouth or ear) which can help them pick sensation up, there may be part of them that thinks or critiques this, *and* then there is part of them observing these thoughts and sensations. 'As you hear/taste X, notice X, notice what thoughts might come up, notice that you are noticing these thoughts and sensations.' It might then be helpful to draw this out for the person.

I have previously done this as a solar system, their observing self at the centre, with orbiting sensations and thoughts. Keeping this visual representation of self-as-context in the session can be helpful in prompting people to recognise thoughts and emotions as they arise, and any common themes (or frames of reference).

It is important to be open with the person that this can be difficult to grasp initially and requires time and effort to practise. As with other experiential exercises, normalising the difficulty of this process can be supported by asking loved ones to practise alongside where appropriate.

Some practical recommendations for ABI populations

As noted above, ACT interventions benefit from being patient-centred, considering the strengths and weaknesses of the individual. Specific adaptations may be necessary, but there are also common recommendations for adaptation in ABI populations. Whiting and colleagues (2017) reviewed research investigating psychological flexibility and cognitive flexibility after traumatic brain injury. They helpfully summarised modifications to support brain injury populations in therapy, and ACT specifically. A key recommendation across therapies was to spend time in initial sessions focusing on educating, normalising and validating.

Other recommendations for modifying support include acknowledging necessary adjustments to support cognitive impairments, such as shortening length of the sessions; using memory aids (e.g. written notes, cue cards, recordings); simplification of tasks; structured session content; increased frequency of sessions; repetition and slowed presentation; and summarising and reviewing content regularly. Whiting and colleagues (2017) also highlighted the importance of providing concrete examples and experiential exercises and being directive in discussions. This links with the recommendation around structure in sessions, but also modelling to patients when practising the skills. ACT-specific recommendations maintained the above, and included trying to develop personally relevant and concrete metaphors; allowing clients to develop their own meaning from metaphors; engaging in experiential exercises, including role playing; and using cognitive techniques that are concrete, such as physicalising the thought (Hayes *et al.*, 1999).

These practical recommendations can be brought into a formulation for how best to introduce and work with self-as-context, combining broader issues, such as adjustment, denial, systems around the individual and cognitive impairment, including 'self-awareness'.

EXAMPLE CASE STUDY

Miles is a 39-year-old man who suffered a left middle cerebral artery stroke around two years ago. Following his stroke, Miles received a great deal of support from speech and language therapy, who noted mild receptive and moderate expressive aphasia, which they felt was unlikely to noticeably improve. He was referred to neuropsychology in a community stroke and neuro-rehab team. He had reported low mood and concerns around changes in his memory and attention. Attention and executive-function related memory difficulties were identified in neuropsychology assessment.

Miles described himself as someone who had worked hard to become a project manager for several engineering companies. He had been recently shortlisted for a new role in Australia, when he suffered the stroke playing football at a weekend with his friends.

Immediately following stroke, he struggled with language, and right visual field loss. Visual field loss dissipated, although dysphasia remained. He received speech and language support in hospital, but little else. After returning home, Miles attempted to return to work, though struggled to manage this and was 'let go' from work as he reported struggling to verbalise instructions to employees.

He was married, with three children, and said that he believed he and his wife would likely separate, as they had grown apart in recent years. His wife agreed the couple had grown apart following the stroke and had almost separated on several occasions. She also described the financial impact that Miles' change in job role had meant for the family, although found it hard to voice her distress, as 'it wasn't [his] fault'. She felt this had changed the relationship, and the life she had envisaged for herself and her children.

For Miles, he believed that the stroke had meant he was unable to do what he 'was meant to do'; which he believed was to work in a high-powered job, be a husband and dad, and be the quick witted and funny sociable person he felt he was pre-stroke.

Following feedback of the cognitive assessment, Miles was reluctant to use any compensation strategies, particularly around asking people to slow down in conversation or tell people he had difficulties with processing information. He said he felt stupid doing this, and it 'wasn't him'. He described being optimistic at times that his difficulties would improve.

Our self-as-context work

Following neuropsychology assessment, Miles consented to therapeutic sessions. We began by using the triflex (i.e. discussing the functional units of Being Present, Opening Up and Doing What Matters). We spoke about awareness of thoughts and feelings and being present in the moment and clarified the concept of mindfulness (he had heard the term, but had some misconceptions).

We spoke about self-as-context from the beginning in our sessions, initially using the metaphor of the mountain and the weather around it, and asking him to 'notice-you-are-noticing'. We worked to create therapeutic safety and compassion, and grounding in the present moment to recognise his thinking self and noticing his thoughts and emotions.

Miles increased his confidence in being active in the session, and was able to build and adapt the metaphor to think about how he had watched his favourite team for many years from the stands. He noted how he had changed stands and seats over the years, and the players, managers and training staff had all changed over the years too. We spoke about how his self-concepts and self-identities, and the thoughts, beliefs, memories and so on, could be thought of as the football players, with the observing-self watching from the stands, able to move seats to get different perspectives. We used this to think about how there may have been times when there were big changes in the team, or he had good or bad seats. We also used this in thinking about how he and someone close (his wife) may watch the game and have different perspectives or focus on different aspects, but still were both fans.

He used a keyring with the emblem of his football team as a token to help him think about that observing self, spectator or fan. He kept this on his house keys and car keys, so saw it often. His wife joined us for part of this first session to discuss the triflex and to think about ways they both could become fused with ideas about Miles' expectations of self-concepts, and we offered his wife space to try using the experiential exercises around noticing and observing thoughts and feelings with us.

We then used pictures and personally meaningful objects to think about how Miles' self-concepts and roles had changed over time. In meeting him at his house, we could use photos and items round the house to talk about how he physically had changed in different contexts from early pictures of him with friends, to him getting married, having kids and so on, while still having a sense of self, or observing self, as a thread through his life.

As we developed safety, compassion and rapport, we spoke more in sessions about the impact of the stroke. Miles had often said that he assumed his speech would continue to improve, and that his cognitive difficulties too would 'get better with time'. When we spoke about the feedback he had received from speech and language therapy that this may not be the case, he could be dismissive. We formulated this as primarily distress and denial around the impact of the stroke, and a way of preserving identity, but at the cost of meaningful activity and relationships in the present.

We introduced the Y-shaped model to reflect on the separation between his experiences now, worries about disability, and the 'ideal' he held in mind that he wanted to return to in the future. We spoke about the costs and benefits of putting effort into reducing activities, and feelings of discrepancy. We wrote this down, rather like a Mental Capacity Act best-interest decision framework of pros and cons. This was a very emotional session, but helped emphasise that he was moving further away from what he valued and was often finding himself caught in thinking (or 'in the game') rather than able to observe this as thoughts and feelings.

We spoke about how his language and the system around him had framed him. We practised using self-as-context experiential observing exercises and defusion exercises, to recognise and respond to emotions when he tried new or triggering activities (such as reaching out to friends, or talking to strangers). We spoke about graded work around who he could reach out to, starting sport again, and spending time with his wife, which linked to his values.

We built on the football-fan metaphor to think about how he found games more enjoyable when he was watching with friends, and watching and talking with others could help him change perspective or have his attention drawn to other aspects of the game. We could write down some of the emotions and thoughts that arose in a game (fear, disappointment, excitement, joy) and use these as prompts for noticing emotions and thoughts he may get caught in day to day.

Miles reflected that being around friends, being physically active and feeling he was learning was always helpful. He committed to arranging times to meet friends, joining his local gym, and date nights with his wife.

Summary

Self-as-context can be a complex concept to introduce into working with people following ABI. However, when done in a sensitive way, tailored to the person, the concept can really help create an important new perspective, and the ability to develop a greater sense of flexibility to approach life following ABI.

References

Beadle, E. J., Ownsworth, T., Fleming, J. & Shum, D. (2016). The impact of traumatic brain injury on self-identity: A systematic review of the evidence for self-concept changes. *The Journal of Head Trauma Rehabilitation*, 31(2), E12–E25.

Bivona, U., Formisano, R., De Laurentiis, S., Accetta, N. *et al.* (2015). Theory of mind impairment after severe traumatic brain injury and its relationship with caregivers' quality of life. *Restorative Neurology and Neuroscience*, 33(3), 335–345.

Cameron, E., Oliver, M. A. & Curvis, W. (2021). Acceptance and Commitment Therapy for People with Moderate or Severe Brain Injuries. In W. Curvis & A. Methley (eds), *Acceptance and Commitment Therapy and Brain Injury* (pp.53–69). London: Routledge.

Cantor, J. B., Ashman, T. A., Schwartz, M. E., Gordon, W.A..(2005). The role of self-discrepancy theory in understanding post-traumatic brain injury affective disorders: a pilot study. *Journal of head trauma rehabilitation, 20*(6), 527–543.

Chesnel, C., Jourdan, C., Bayen, E., Ghout, I. *et al.* (2018). Self-awareness four years after severe traumatic brain injury: Discordance between the patient's and relative's complaints. Results from the PariS-TBI study. *Clinical Rehabilitation,* 32(5), 692–704.

Choi, I. & Choi, Y. (2002). Culture and self-concept flexibility. *Personality and Social Psychology Bulletin,* 28(11), 1508–1517.

Crosson, B., Barco, P. P., Velozo, C. A., Bolesta, M. *et al.* (1989). Awareness and compensation in postacute head injury rehabilitation. *The Journal of Head Trauma Rehabilitation,* 4(3), 46–54.

DeAndrea, D. C., Shaw, A. S. & Levine, T. R. (2010). Online language: The role of culture in self-expression and self-construal on Facebook. *Journal of Language and Social Psychology,* 29(4), 425–442.

Foody, M., Barnes-Holmes, Y., Barnes-Holmes, D. & Luciano, C. (2013). An empirical investigation of hierarchical versus distinction relations in a self-based ACT exercise. *International Journal of Psychology and Psychological Therapy,* 13(3), 373–388.

Fleming, J. M., Strong, J. & Ashton, R. (1996). Self-awareness of deficits in adults with traumatic brain injury: How best to measure? *Brain Injury,* 10(1), 1–16.

Geytenbeek, M., Fleming, J., Doig, E. & Ownsworth, T. (2017). The occurrence of early impaired self-awareness after traumatic brain injury and its relationship with emotional distress and psychosocial functioning. *Brain Injury,* 31(13–14), 1791–1798.

Godbee, M. & Kangas, M. (2020). The relationship between flexible perspective taking and emotional well-being: A systematic review of the 'self-as-context' component of acceptance and commitment therapy. *Behavior Therapy,* 51(6), 917–932.

Gracey, F., Evans, J. J. & Malley, D. (2009). Capturing process and outcome in complex rehabilitation interventions: A 'Y-shaped' model. *Neuropsychological Rehabilitation,* 19(6), 867–890.

Gracey, F., Vicentijevic, K. & Methley, A. (2021). The Y-Shaped model of psychological adaptation after brain injury: An acceptance and commitment perspective. In W. Curvis & A. Methley (eds), *Acceptance and Commitment Therapy and Brain Injury* (pp.16–25). London: Routledge.

Harris, R. (2009). *ACT Made Simple: An Easy-to-Read Primer on Acceptance and Commitment Therapy* (first edition). Oakland, CA: New Harbinger Publications.

Harris, R. (2019). *ACT Made Simple: An Easy-to-Read Primer on Acceptance and Commitment Therapy* (second edition). Oakland, CA: New Harbinger Publications.

Hayes, S. C., Strosahl, K. D. & Wilson, K. G. (2011). *Acceptance and Commitment Therapy: An Experiential Approach to Behavior Change.* New York, NY: Guilford Press.

Higgins, E. T., Klein, R. & Strauman, T. (1985). Self-concept discrepancy theory: A psychological model for distinguishing among different aspects of depression and anxiety. *Social Cognition,* 3(1), 51–76.

Jeffay E, Ponsford J, Harnett A, et al. (2023). INCOG 2.0 guidelines for cognitive rehabilitation following traumatic brain injury, part III: executive functions. *J Head Trauma Rehabilitation,* 38(1):52–64.

Kangas, M. & McDonald, S. (2011). Is it time to act? The potential of acceptance and commitment therapy for psychological problems following acquired brain injury. *Neuropsychological Rehabilitation,* 21(2), 250–276.

Mamman, R. M. (2022). *Life with Traumatic Brain Injury: Experiences of Social Participation, Self-Awareness, and Self-Identity* (Doctoral dissertation, University of British Columbia).

Miller, W. R. & Rollnick, S. (2012). *Motivational Interviewing: Helping People Change*. New York, NY: Guilford Press.

Nochi, M. (1998). 'Loss of self' in the narratives of people with traumatic brain injuries: A qualitative analysis. *Social Science & Medicine*, 46(7), 869–878.

Nochi, M. (2000). Reconstructing self-narratives in coping with traumatic brain injury. *Social Science & Medicine*, 51(12), 1795–1804.

O'Callaghan, C., Powell, T. & Oyebode, J. (2006). An exploration of the experience of gaining awareness of deficit in people who have suffered a traumatic brain injury. *Neuropsychological Rehabilitation*, 16(5), 579–593.

Oh, W. (2022). Understanding of self: Buddhism and psychoanalysis. *Journal of Religion and Health*, 61(6), 4696–4707.

Ownsworth, T. (2014). *Self-Identity After Brain Injury*. Brighton, UK: Psychology Press.

Prigatano, G. P. (1999). *Principles of Neuropsychological Rehabilitation*. New York, NY: Oxford University Press.

Prigatano, G. P. (2012). Anosognosia, denial, and other disorders of phenomenological experience. *Acta Neuropsychologica*, 10(3), 371–384.

Prigatano, G. P. & Sherer, M. (2020). Impaired self-awareness and denial during the postacute phases after moderate to severe traumatic brain injury. *Frontiers in Psychology*, 11, 1569.

Robertson, K. & Schmitter-Edgecombe, M. (2015). Self-awareness and traumatic brain injury outcome. *Brain Injury*, 29(7–8), 848–858.

Sabat, S. R. & Harré, R. (1992). The construction and deconstruction of self in Alzheimer's disease. *Ageing & Society*, 12(4), 443–461.

Sansonetti, D., Fleming, J., Patterson, F. & Lannin, N. A. (2022). Conceptualization of self-awareness in adults with acquired brain injury: A qualitative systematic review. *Neuropsychological Rehabilitation*, 32(8), 1726–1773.

Skidmore, E. R., Swafford, M., Juengst, S. B. & Terhorst, L. (2018). Self-awareness and recovery of independence with strategy training. *The American Journal of Occupational Therapy*, 72(1), 1–5.

Sutton, A. (2016). Measuring the effects of self-awareness: Construction of the self-awareness outcomes questionnaire. *Europe's Journal of Psychology*, 12(4), 645.

Toglia, J. & Kirk, U. (2000). Understanding awareness deficits following brain injury. *NeuroRehabilitation*, 15(1), 57–70.

Toglia, J., & Maeir, Y. (2018). Self-awareness and metacognition. In N. Katz & J. Toglia (Eds.). *Cognition, occupation, and participation across the life span: neuroscience, neurorehabilitation, and models of intervention in OT*. Bethesda, MD: AOTA Press.

Vignoles, V. L., Owe, E., Becker, M., Smith, P. B. *et al.* (2016). Beyond the 'east–west' dichotomy: Global variation in cultural models of selfhood. *Journal of Experimental Psychology: General*, 145(8), 966.

Westrup, D. (2014). *Advanced Acceptance and Commitment Therapy: The Experienced Practitioner's Guide to Optimizing Delivery*. Oakland, CA: New Harbinger Publications.

Whiting, D., Simpson, G., Ciarrochi, J. & McLeod, H. (2012). Assessing the feasibility of Acceptance and Commitment Therapy in promoting psychological adjustment after severe traumatic brain injury. *Brain Injury*, 26(4–5), 558–559.

Whiting, D. L., Deane, F. P., Simpson, G. K., McLeod, H. J. & Ciarrochi, J. (2017). Cognitive and psychological flexibility after a traumatic brain injury and the implications for treatment in acceptance-based therapies: A conceptual review. *Neuropsychological Rehabilitation*, 27(2), 263–299.

Willig, C. (2012). *Qualitative Interpretation and Analysis in Psychology*. London: McGraw-Hill Education.

Yeates, G. N., Henwood, K., Gracey, F., & Evans, J. (2007). Awareness of disability after ABI and the family context. *Neuropsychological rehabilitation*, 17(2), 151–173.

Ylvisaker, M., Mcpherson, K., Kayes, N. & Pellett, E. (2008). Metaphoric identity mapping: Facilitating goal setting and engagement in rehabilitation after traumatic brain injury. *Neuropsychological Rehabilitation*, 18(5–6), 713–741.

Yu, L., McCracken, L. M. & Norton, S. (2016). The Self Experiences Questionnaire (SEQ): Preliminary analyses for a measure of self in people with chronic pain. *Journal of Contextual Behavioral Science*, 5(3), 127–133.

Zettle, R. D., Gird, S. R., Webster, B. K., Carrasquillo-Richardson, N., Swails, J. A. & Burdsal, C. A. (2018). The Self-as-Context Scale: Development and preliminary psychometric properties. *Journal of Contextual Behavioral Science*, 10, 64–74.

CHAPTER 6

Values and Valued Living with Acquired Brain Injury

DANA WONG AND NICK SATHANANTHAN

About the authors and their work

This chapter focuses on a topic that is important and meaningful to both of us. We are clinical neuropsychologists, researchers and educators who work with adults with acquired brain injury and illness (ABI), including stroke, traumatic brain injury, hypoxic brain injury, brain tumour and multiple sclerosis. We will therefore be focusing on these conditions throughout the chapter. Nick Sathananthan has completed a master's degree in clinical neuropsychology and is currently completing his doctorate, focusing on the development and evaluation of the VaLiANT (Valued Living After Neurological Trauma) group programme, which combines cognitive rehabilitation and ACT techniques to enhance valued living and meaningful participation after ABI (Sathananthan *et al.*, 2021, 2022).

Dana Wong is Nick's supervisor and has been working in ABI rehabilitation research and practice since the early 2000s. Her aim is to strengthen the evidence base for cognitive and psychological interventions to improve quality of life post-ABI and translate these into practice by training clinicians to competently deliver those interventions.

Values are our beliefs and principles about what is important in life and are enduring guides to our actions. Over the last 15 years, my (Dana's) clinical and research work in psychological interventions for people with acquired brain injury using cognitive behaviour therapy – adapted for brain injury (CBT-ABI) (Wong *et al.*, 2019) increasingly confirmed to me the importance of identifying and working with values as drivers for behaviour change in a person-centred care framework. This was illustrated by our work evaluating the relationship between valued living (values-based action) and improved functional and psychosocial outcomes after traumatic brain injury (Pais *et al.*, 2019; Pais-Hrit *et al.*, 2020), which we subsequently replicated in a broader sample of adults with stroke and other ABIs (Armstrong *et al.*, 2020). This work highlighted the importance of targeting valued living in rehabilitation interventions aimed at improving meaningful participation, wellbeing and quality of life following ABI, which then led to the development of VaLiANT (Sathananthan *et al.*, 2021).

During the initial single case experimental design evaluation of VaLiANT (Sathananthan *et al.*, 2021), we noticed some issues with measuring valued living accurately with participants with cognitive and communication difficulties, particularly when using the Valued Living Questionnaire (VLQ). We therefore decided to conduct a cognitive interviewing study evaluating how people with ABI were understanding the items on the VLQ. We found that 11 common comprehension errors were made by people with ABI (Miller *et al.*, 2022), discussed further in the section on adaptations in this chapter. In response to these findings, we developed a revised version of the VLQ which we called the VLQ-Comprehension Support version (VLQ-CS), using communication support principles to improve accessibility and re-structuring the questionnaire to address the source of the common comprehension errors (see the Resources section of the chapter). The VLQ-CS has now been validated in 103 people with ABI (Wong, Miller *et al.*, under review) and in 70 neurotypical adults (Skaliotis *et al.*, in preparation). We have also characterised which values are most important to people with ABI, as identified on both the VLQ-CS and a values card sort task, and compared these with a neurotypical cohort (Wong, Lynch *et al.*, 2025). Findings highlighted the importance to people both with and without ABI of health and wellbeing, and relationships with family, children and spouses/partners.

Our research, on which we elaborate in subsequent sections, has demonstrated the importance of targeting valued living in rehabilitation and interventions for people with ABI, and using methods and measures for identifying and monitoring values and valued living that are suited to people with cognitive and communication difficulties, to ensure that values-based interventions are appropriately targeted and outcomes are measured accurately. More accessible interventions and measures of values and valued living can also benefit neurotypical and other clinical populations. We hope that this book chapter can guide values-based practice in a way that optimises its benefits for people living with ABI and other neurological conditions.

Chapter overview

This chapter includes the following:

- The importance of values for people with neurological conditions, including the potential ways in which interventions targeting valued living may be beneficial for people with ABI.

- Adaptations to values-based measures, interventions and techniques for people with ABI, including improvements to the accessibility of measurement tools of values and valued living, and adaptations that can be made to ACT-based interventions.

- Two case studies, describing values-based work with one of the participants in our VaLiANT group intervention, and with an ABI rehabilitation team.

- Resources for the assessment of values and valued living.

The importance of values for people with neurological conditions

Living a meaningful life with purpose is central to human wellbeing. Meaning in life is underpinned by connection to core values, pursuit of purposeful behaviour in line with these values, and continuity of self-identity over time so that the past self, present self and future self are connected (King & Hicks, 2021; Mulahalilović *et al.*, 2021). For example, someone may have a core value around helping others, so they pursue paid and volunteer work in helping professions, and their past, present and future identity are connected by these roles and ongoing actions to help others. However, valued action and self-continuity represent some of the key areas that are disrupted by ABI. Change to self-identity is frequently reported and is often represented by a negative evaluation of the current self in comparison to the pre-injury self (Emery *et al.*, 2022; Gracey, Evans & Malley, 2009). Similarly, engagement in valued activities and life roles that provide a sense of purpose are also frequently impacted, with many individuals struggling to return to their pre-injury life roles (Fadyl *et al.*, 2019; Pais *et al.*, 2019).

These changes are largely caused by the presence of persistent physical, cognitive, emotional and behavioural symptoms which place new restrictions on what is possible. As an example, cognitive impairment and mood disturbance affect over half of individuals with acquired brain injury and independently predict reduced participation in work, leisure and social activities up to ten years after injury (Draper, Ponsford & Schönberger, 2007; Stolwyk *et al.*, 2021; Theadom *et al.*, 2018). These impacts can cause a fundamental loss of meaning and purpose in life. For the person with the core value of helping others, an ABI may result in cognitive and physical limitations that prevent them from engaging in their previous paid and volunteer roles and place them in a position where they are the recipient rather than the provider of help. Those living with ABI have described the experience of trying to regain meaning in life as uncertain and challenging, with many describing a lack of direction linked with ongoing difficulties with adjusting to the ABI (Jumisko, Lexell & Söderberg, 2005; Shipley *et al.*, 2018).

Techniques that can facilitate adjustment and reconstruction of what gives life meaning are therefore much needed for people living with ABI (Vaghela, Santoro & Braham, 2021). Values can play a key role in guiding this process of adjustment. Values are defined as chosen courses of purposive action that are dynamic and evolving, distinguishable from goals with achievable ends (Hayes *et al.*, 2006; Wilson *et al.*, 2010). A key aim of ACT is to increase psychological flexibility while also facilitating exploration of values and increasing values-guided action or valued living. As described by Hayes, Strosahl and Wilson (2012, p.13), 'all ACT techniques are eventually subordinated to helping the client live in accord with his or her chosen values', positioning valued living as a primary outcome from therapy. There is an increasing body of evidence associating valued living with positive outcomes for a range of different conditions. Higher levels of valued living have been associated with lower psychological distress and better quality of life and functioning in clinical populations without neurological damage, such as those with chronic pain (McCracken & Yang, 2006) and mood disorders (Michelson *et al.*, 2011; Smout *et al.*, 2014).

These relationships are also evident following ABI, where higher levels of valued living are associated with better functional outcomes, such as being more likely to return to work, and lower psychological distress (Baseotto *et al.*, 2022; Pais *et al.*, 2019). Valued living has been shown to be reduced from pre-injury levels for at least 12–36 months following brain injury, which likely reflects a reduced ability to pursue previously valued activities, and ongoing difficulties with the development of new valued behaviours (Pais *et al.*, 2019). Intervention studies targeting valued living following ABI have resulted in improvements to quality of life and mood in those with multiple sclerosis (Sheppard *et al.*, 2010), and the evidence supporting ACT as an intervention for psychological distress following traumatic brain injury is accumulating (Sander *et al.*, 2021; Whiting *et al.*, 2020). Stroke survivors have also described improved meaningful activity following a brief ACT intervention, despite ongoing post-stroke symptoms (Majumdar & Morris, 2019). Our preliminary single-case experimental evaluation indicated that an eight-week group valued living intervention (VaLiANT) may also improve wellbeing, quality of life and acceptance following ABI (Sathananthan *et al.*, 2021). Our recent qualitative evaluation of VaLiANT supported these findings, suggesting that addressing cognitive and psychological barriers to valued living and connecting with others post-ABI led to identity reconstruction or 'finding the me I can be' (Sathananthan *et al.*, 2024). These studies highlight that promotion of valued activity following ABI could be a key mechanism for improving holistic, person-centred outcomes like adjustment and reconstruction of identity and meaning.

There are several possible mechanisms underpinning the link between valued living and identity reconstruction following ABI. First, it is possible that valued living increases opportunities and contexts for meaningful behaviours linked with positive self-identity. Better engagement in valued activities and life roles following ABI has been linked to more positive appraisal of self-identity, while lack of engagement in valued activities is associated with negative appraisals of self-identity (Fraas & Calvert, 2009; Lennon *et al.*, 2014). The capacity to engage in meaningful activity may give individuals a greater sense of control in life despite the presence of difficult symptoms (Arch & Craske, 2008). Second, re-engagement in the pursuit of meaningful goals that are feasible following ABI has been shown to reduce distress, which may in turn improve psychological flexibility (through recognising that a greater range of meaningful behaviours is possible) and acceptance of the brain injury, and lead to higher quality of life (Scobbie *et al.*, 2021; Van Bost, Van Damme & Crombez, 2020). Finally, improvements in valued living have also been associated with improvements in post-traumatic growth (Baseotto *et al.*, 2022; Pais-Hrit *et al.*, 2020). Post-traumatic growth refers to a process in which some individuals respond to a traumatic event (in this case, an ABI) in a way that enables them to identify some benefit from their experience and make positive changes in their psychological or behavioural functioning as a result (McGrath, 2004). It frequently follows a 'search for meaning' triggered by the traumatic event (Pais-Hrit *et al.*, 2020) and is often represented by a deeper understanding of one's self and reorganisation of priorities, which conceptually overlaps with values and valued living. Behaviours considered indicative of post-traumatic growth (e.g. spending more time with family and friends, greater involvement in community groups, increased appreciation of nature) can be conceived as forms of valued living (Baseotto *et al.*, 2022; Pais *et al.*, 2019).

Therefore, the process of exploring values and generating new valued behaviours may help people recognise a change in values following ABI (e.g. higher prioritisation of family over work), or demonstrate that their values have not changed but their pre-injury behaviour was not aligned to their values (e.g. they were spending too much time at work and not enough with family), leading to positive psychological and behavioural growth.

Another benefit of targeting values-based behaviour change in interventions for people with ABI is that it inevitably broadens the focus of interventions beyond specific impairments (e.g. cognitive impairment or depression symptoms), instead targeting holistic, person-centred, meaningful outcomes. From the perspective of the person with ABI, this is often a welcome contrast to other experiences of treatment which can be medicalised or symptom focused. As just outlined, values-based interventions can encourage positive growth, not just symptom reduction, fostering a deeper connection with the things that imbue life with meaning, purpose and pleasure.

Values-based interventions also provide a solid framework for rebuilding identity across diverse cultures. While there are cultural differences in the representation and importance of particular values and how these values are enacted through behaviour, this cross-cultural variability is no greater than differences within each culture (Hanel *et al.*, 2018). However, careful attention is needed to explore how values are represented and enacted for each person whose cultural background differs from the practitioner, to ensure that normative ideologies are not being assumed. As an example, Australian Aboriginal and Torres Strait islander people's representations of family can differ significantly from traditional Western notions of the nuclear family, extending beyond immediate blood relatives to also include relationships towards their broader communities under the kinship system (Fejo-King, 2013). This system also incorporates responsibilities towards the land and resources, with associated value-consistent behaviours that might not be considered relevant to family in a Western context. Importantly, however, despite these cultural differences in values representation and behaviour, the benefits of connection with what gives life meaning are trans-cultural.

Adaptations to values-based measures and interventions for people with ABI

A range of adaptations are necessary to traditional assessment and intervention techniques for values and valued living to enhance accessibility and engagement for those with ABI-related changes in cognitive and communication abilities. Cognitive domains commonly affected by ABI incorporate memory, attention, processing speed and executive functions, including abstract reasoning, idea generation, cognitive flexibility and metacognitive awareness. Values work relies heavily on these cognitive abilities. Values and valued living are abstract, complex concepts, and familiarity with these ideas is often limited prior to therapy, both in ABI and the neurotypical population. In ACT research, it has been demonstrated that self-ratings of valued living are high at the beginning of therapy, but then decrease as individuals gain a deeper understanding of their values and the misalignment between their values and actions (Wilson *et al.*, 2010). This represents a process of acculturating to the concepts of values and valued living by reflecting on and applying these ideas in relation to the self. An additional challenge for people with ABI is that traditional values work does not account for changes to self-identity and the disruption of self-continuity that often occurs following ABI. Pre-injury representations of what was important may no longer be relevant. Values identification and linking values to behaviour is therefore a more multi-layered process that needs to account for ABI-related changes to values and values-based actions. It is easy to underestimate the cognitive demands of engaging in this type of work.

The need to adapt commonly used values measures was clearly demonstrated in our research investigating comprehension of the VLQ by people with ABI (Miller *et al.*, 2022), which highlighted numerous conceptual misunderstandings. These included:

- difficulties with the conceptualisation of personal values whereby the importance of value domains was rated based on the perceived societal importance rather than personal importance (e.g. rating education as highly important based on the belief that education is important for society as a whole)

- rating the importance of values based on capacity to engage successfully in behaviours in line with that value (e.g. giving a low rating for the importance of work due to no longer being able to work) or pre-injury importance

- difficulty deciding 'how consistent your actions have been with each of your values' in the past week because of:
  - interpreting 'consistency' as regularity of actions from day to day (e.g. consistently exercising every day) rather than value-consistency (i.e. acting in a way that is consistent with personal values – such as exercising as an action consistent with a value around physical health)
  - difficulty recalling what they had done in the past week
  - difficulty evaluating whether their actions were consistent with values, especially for actions that were part of their usual routine
  - struggling to understand that a lack of activity in a certain life domain would warrant a high consistency rating for value domains rated as low in importance.

These issues are relevant to other commonly used values clarification tasks from ACT. For example, most versions of values card sort tasks used in ACT express values in very general terms, such as 'Forgiveness', 'Love' or 'Health', which provide the person with very little guidance about the nature of that value (e.g. 'Forgiveness' might mean that the person values forgiving others, or being forgiven by others). Similarly, although it appears simple and visually appealing, the 'Values Bullseye' task requires an individual to self-generate their values for four different life domains (work/education, relationships, personal growth/health, leisure) and then to rate how closely they are living in accordance with those values (Lundgren *et al.*, 2012). To self-generate values requires the ability to generate ideas, reason abstractly, self-reflect and comprehend complex verbal concepts. To make accurate evaluations of valued living, the person needs to be able to remember their behaviours, identify behaviours which link to each abstract value and evaluate whether their recent behaviours could be considered value-consistent. This is a challenging task for many people with ABI.

Techniques

There is a clear need for tools and techniques specifically developed or tailored for those with ABI and other conditions affecting cognition and/or communication. Here we have listed some of the key adaptations we made in the VLQ-CS and in the values card sort and other values-based activities we use in the VaLiANT programme. Broadly, these adaptations can be categorised as improving 1) accurate measurement of personal values and valued living, 2) the clarity of explanations of the concept of values and 3) exploration of behaviour change in line with values over the course of intervention.

1. Accurate measurement of values and valued living

The adaptations made in the VLQ-CS (full version is included in the Resources section) (Wong, Miller *et al.*, under review) included both general strategies previously established to improve accessibility of materials for people with ABI, and specific revisions to address the comprehension errors identified in our cognitive interviewing study (Miller *et al.*, 2022). General strategies included visual aids to support comprehension of written material, simplification and inbuilt repetition of instructions, and concrete examples of abstract concepts. These are some specific revisions made to address common comprehension issues:

- Changing instructions to emphasise current (post-ABI) personal importance rather than societal importance ('How important is [domain] *to you at the moment?*').

- Replacing the term 'consistency' with a scale of 'not ideal at all' (1) to 'ideal' (10), in response to the question 'In the last week, how much quality time or effort have you spent on [domain]?' This frames 'consistency' more clearly by making the comparator 'the ideal'.

- Providing several examples of value-consistent actions (together with pictures of those actions) to scaffold the evaluation of whether actions in the past week have been consistent with values.

- Altering the structure so questions about importance and consistency for each domain immediately follow one another.

- Changing administration instructions so that if a value 4 or less is selected for the importance rating, consistency is not rated for that domain.

2. Clearly explaining values

When introducing values in the VaLiANT programme, we use the metaphor of travelling north but never 'arriving' at north as analogous to valued directions, which are then differentiated from goals, which are likened to destinations. Facilitators then give examples from their own lives to bring this concept to life; for example, I (Dana) might say that one of my values is to be a loving parent, and that when I hug my children goodnight tonight, that does not mean I have then 'ticked off' that value and no longer need to take active steps towards it.

We then show slides with pictures and descriptions of famous people (e.g. Princess Diana, Steve Irwin, Donald Trump) and ask group participants to identify values they think are important to those people. A follow-up question, 'What do you think they care most about?', is included if needed. This typically generates discussion around which values are likely to be driving their actions. The final picture is of a member of the ABI community (shared with his permission) whose stroke at a young age prevented him from pursuing his career in musical theatre. Instead, he developed an online platform for neurotrauma survivors to share their stories, as an alternative way to act in accordance with his value of telling stories to shed light on the human experience. This serves to demonstrate the idea that valued living remains possible after ABI, even though the specific values-based actions may be different.

3. Exploring values and values-consistent behaviours throughout intervention

As a general principle, repetition and consolidation of values-based activities is important. In VaLiANT, values card sort or other values clarification activities are completed in every session. For some participants, particularly those with more severe cognitive impairments, full understanding of the valued living concept is only achieved towards the end of the programme, reflecting the time and repetition needed to acculturate to values work.

After explaining the concept of values, values clarification for the individual with ABI is an important next step that can help restore the continuity of self either by establishing what remains the same from pre- to post-injury or by highlighting how the experience of ABI has changed values. In the first session, participants sort an overall set of values covering all key life domains, and then in subsequent sessions they sort more specific values relevant to the life domain that is the topic for that session (e.g. Relationships/connecting with others). We developed our own set of values cards (see Resources section) where each value is phrased as a direction for action (e.g. 'to earn respect from others') rather than a broad abstract word or phrase (e.g. 'respect'). Each value phrase is accompanied by a relevant picture to support comprehension of the value (e.g. a photo of a handshake). These communication support strategies provide scaffolding to encourage participants to make the link between their values and actions. Participants sort the cards into three piles ('Very important to me', 'Important to me' and 'Not important to me') and then choose their top five most important values from the 'Very important to me' pile. This card sort format is visually and physically engaging and facilitates decision-making about which values are most important to them.

When values have been identified and the life domains that are most important are clarified, a framework to guide behaviour change can then be built. For example, if 'being a good parent' is identified as one of the most important values for an individual, actions and behaviours in line with this (e.g. spending time playing with their children) can be planned. Identifying which goals or areas of life are priorities is particularly important when interpersonal resources are more limited (e.g. due to fatigue) as fewer tasks or activities can be achieved each day. Linking values to new specific actions can help increase the intrinsic reward of these behaviours and improve engagement and behavioural adjustment even though the behaviour might be quite different from pre-injury (e.g. working in a part-time voluntary role compared with previous full-time paid work).

In the VaLiANT intervention, after identifying important values in a specific life domain (e.g. health), participants select one that they would like to work towards during that week. Participants are then supported to complete The Way to Valued Living worksheet where they identify up to three SMART (Specific, Measurable, Achievable, Relevant, Time-bound) goals or actions to complete that week in line with their chosen value (e.g. going for a 20-minute walk every morning – as shown in the example worksheet in the Resources section). This can be a difficult process, with participants often needing directive guidance to identify feasible actions that are relevant to their chosen value. Participants can struggle to identify goals or become stuck on goals that are too 'big', vague or unrelated to their chosen value. This requires a skilled facilitator to guide or redirect the participant by suggesting specific goals or actions that they believe will be relevant and achievable for the participant, based on a comprehensive case formulation. Participants are then taught cognitive and psychological strategies to enable them to achieve their weekly goals.

Comprehensive homework review is another essential element supporting the consolidation of values work over the course of the intervention. This serves to encourage accountability, identify barriers to achievement of their weekly values-based action and guide implementation of strategies to address those barriers (e.g. using memory aids). Importantly, guided reflections on the experience of acting in line with their values can also enhance self-awareness and highlight whether each values-based action is experienced as genuinely rewarding or meaningful (Barney *et al.*, 2019). If indeed it is, reflecting on that experience is likely to encourage the behaviour to continue. It can also lead to re-appraisal of regular existing behaviours as value-consistent, which may in turn lead them to be experienced as more meaningful or enjoyable. If values-based actions are not experienced as rewarding, this may reflect issues with the process of identifying important values or values-based actions, for example due to the influence of social desirability or norms (e.g. a mother may feel an expectation to rate parenting as more important to her than it actually is, leading her to identify goals that are not experienced as fundamentally rewarding). Uncovering this with an open, non-judgemental stance can unlock deeper reflections on what is truly important to the individual.

CASE STUDIES: VALUES-BASED WORK WITH INDIVIDUALS, GROUPS AND TEAMS

To illustrate values-based work in action, we present one individual and one brief team case study.

Case 1

Elaine (name changed) is a 59-year-old woman who participated in the VaLiANT group programme, which incorporates ACT techniques with cognitive rehabilitation to enhance valued living (Sathananthan *et al.*, 2021, 2022). Elaine presented with cognitive and emotional changes after a right-sided subcortical ischaemic stroke and then a right-sided internal capsule haemorrhage six months later. The strokes resulted in executive dysfunction, increased emotional sensitivity and persistent fatigue. These symptoms were impacting her daily functioning and meaningful participation. She struggled to complete complex tasks (e.g. following cooking recipes), was forgetful and no longer felt confident in managing her day. As a result, she was not spending as much time caring for her grandchildren, which was an important life role for her. Her partner had significant pre-existing mental health difficulties which placed strain on their relationship and Elaine had withdrawn from her social network since her strokes. Her work hours, responsibilities and performance were also impacted due to losing track of conversations, struggling to retain information, and fatigue. Prior to the strokes she was seeking a promotion; however, this was no longer considered possible.

Elaine's goals centred around improving her daily functioning and management of symptoms to enable her to continue working while also being able to take care of her grandchildren. On the values card sort task conducted in the first session, she identified her five most important values as being 'to look after my physical health', 'to look after my mental health', 'to feel good about myself', 'to play and have fun' and 'to be a loving family member', reflecting the importance she placed on health, wellbeing and family. In group discussions, Elaine also expressed a sense of grief around her difficulties in the workplace. It was evident that the changes to her confidence to perform key life roles were significantly impacting her mood, self-worth and identity.

The second and third sessions of the VaLiANT programme focus on health (sleep/fatigue in the second session, and diet/exercise in the third). In these sessions, Elaine noted that she often ate unhealthy snacks, especially at times where she was feeling fatigued, and she wanted to change this habit. In the third session, Elaine participated in the 'passengers on the bus' group exercise, in which she was the driver who was trying to drive her 'bus of life' towards the value of 'looking after my physical health', while the passengers were voicing all the reasons to drive in a different direction or stop driving altogether. In the process of doing the exercise, Elaine realised that the pursuit of health-related values was actually driven by her deeper underlying values around family and wanting to be healthy and active for her grandchildren. This was a key moment of values clarification for Elaine. This realisation provided a new source of motivation for changing health behaviours, leading her to stick a picture of her grandchildren on her refrigerator to remind her of the values guiding her actions before she decided on what to eat.

In the session focusing on work, Elaine expressed ongoing workplace difficulties and frustration at her boss not accommodating her support needs. For The Way to Valued Living worksheet for that week, her chosen 'goals and actions' focused on family and leisure rather than her workplace. This represented another shift whereby Elaine began to focus more on recreational activities than work, reflecting re-prioritisation of value domains. Throughout the remainder of the programme, Elaine chose to spend her time focusing on looking after herself to ensure her longevity for her family, and on enjoying life and planning leisure activities. In the final session, Elaine acknowledged that there was a likelihood of her job being terminated, but she was not nearly as concerned about that as was previously, and acknowledged that she wanted to spend more time on creative art pursuits.

In a semi-structured interview eight weeks after the programme (for the purposes of our qualitative evaluation of VaLiANT), Elaine commented: 'For me, learning that having fun is more important than work has been really valuable, especially because I'm not working now. Not through my choice. Because I've stopped work, valuing and doing art has given me a direction. VaLiANT got me more valuing family and realising that for me to be valued to family, I've got to look after me. I'm really trying my best to look after me, my health. Doing the physical stuff, I know it's important. Even the other day I was cold and miserable, but I pushed myself to go for my walk. Even though I don't feel like it sometimes.' When reflecting on the values card sort task, she said, 'It showed me what I found was important in my life because I was, a lot, thinking about work being important. I think I've realised that family is more important and having fun is more important than work.'

Elaine's case highlights how clarification of important personal values can be crucial for meaningfully guiding behaviour change. The links between behavioural goals (e.g. eating healthier snacks) and the deeper values underpinning these goals are not always obvious. In Elaine's case, it was plausible that 'to look after my physical health' was the most relevant value, but this was an insufficient reason for her to change her eating habits, perhaps because it felt too self-focused. Uncovering the underlying value of caring for her grandchildren allowed her to give herself permission to look after herself, as it was in the service of others. Elaine's case also highlights that re-prioritising of values and re-conceptualising what valued living looks like in terms of clear, achievable, concrete everyday actions post-ABI are central to identity re-construction. For her, work was an important part of her pre-injury identity; but her cognitive and emotional changes led her to place greater emphasis on fun and leisure, shaping her post-injury identity. It is also evident that Elaine's psychological distress in relation to not being able to work was reduced through re-engagement in other valued behaviours, exemplifying the underlying mechanisms linking valued living to better adjustment and acceptance discussed earlier in the chapter. Generating weekly committed actions was an important part of this process; for example, she decided to buy a whoopee cushion to play a practical joke on her grandchildren as an action consistent with her value 'to play and have fun'. Values work is often an ongoing exploration which evolves as participants become tuned in to what matters most deeply to them. This means that continually revisiting values and how these translate into achievable values-based actions throughout therapy may be an important mechanism driving positive therapy outcomes.

Case 2

The Caulfield ABI team is part of a major publicly funded health service in Melbourne, Australia. It includes inpatient and community-based rehabilitation services as well as a transitional living service to support people with severe ABI to live in the community after hospital discharge. The clients include people with moderate to severe traumatic brain injury, stroke and other acquired brain injury, many of whom have complex comorbid health conditions and social disadvantage. The team has a strong focus on evidence-based practice, embedded clinical research and quality improvement.

This team collaborated on a student project evaluating the relationship between valued living and functional and psychosocial outcomes (Armstrong *et al.*, 2020). As part of this project, the team was shown the VLQ-CS. Subsequently, several team members asked if they were able to use the VLQ-CS in their clinical practice (outside the research). This measure was adopted by the transitional living and community rehabilitation teams and used by some practitioners in their initial assessments with new patients. They provided feedback that the measure was useful in understanding what was most important to their patients and was a helpful tool to guide goal setting. This aligns with the findings of a service evaluation conducted in the UK (Rose & Rendell, 2022), which found that training staff in a severe brain injury unit on how to do values-based goal setting resulted in increased accessibility of goals, and both clinicians and service users reported a positive experience of meaningful goal setting. In the Caulfield ABI setting, the examples of values-based action included in the VLQ-CS were found to be useful examples of how goals may look. As previously discussed, generating goals can be challenging after ABI, particularly in the context of impairments in idea generation, planning and organisation, and insight and awareness. Providing examples of specific values-based actions in key life domains can trigger ideas for goals and help set directions for multidisciplinary rehabilitation. This highlights potential uses for the VLQ-CS beyond measuring intervention outcomes. It also points to the need for further work generating a 'bank' of values-based goals and actions for all key life domains, which we plan to do as a co-design project with people with lived experience of ABI.

Summary

In this chapter, we have aimed to demonstrate the value of values-based work in people with ABI and other neurological conditions. This work includes supporting our clients to understand the concepts and importance of values and valued living; to clarify which values hold the greatest personal importance to them; to identify feasible, relevant committed actions or goals which reflect those values; and supporting them to achieve those goals. This process of values-based behaviour change can facilitate adjustment to life post-ABI and encourage meaningful identity reconstruction. However, our assessment tools and intervention techniques must be suitable and accessible for people with cognitive and/or communication difficulties post-ABI, which often requires adaptations to the versions used in non-neurological populations. Carefully considered values-based work has the potential to meaningfully improve quality of life for people living with ABl.

Values resources for people with ABI and neurological conditions

This section includes the following resources:

- The administration instructions for the VLQ-CS, including a paper version of the questionnaire, and scoring instructions. We also have an electronic version of the VLQ-CS in REDCap, which is available from the authors on request (email d.wong@latrobe.edu.au).

- The values card sort cards we use in the VaLiANT programme. Together with software developer Hassan Farhat, we have developed an online version of the card sort activities (including the overall version used in Session 1, and the domain-specific versions focusing on Health, Work/Community, Leisure and Relationships). We can make this version freely available for clinicians and researchers to use with people who are willing for their data to be used for research purposes. Please contact d.wong@latrobe.edu.au for further details about accessing the telehealth version.

- The Way to Valued Living worksheet, with a completed example.

A blank version of The Way to Valued Living worksheet and all other materials used in the VaLiANT programme will be included in the treatment manual which we plan to publish not too long after this book is published.

Valued Living Questionnaire – Comprehension Support Version (VLQ-CS): Administration Instructions

The VLQ-CS has been designed to maximise user-friendliness for individuals who have cognitive or communication difficulties (e.g. due to an acquired brain injury). However, the extent to which individuals may need extra assistance and prompting to complete the measure will vary. The guidelines below aim to clarify some difficulties which may arise when assisting someone with cognitive difficulties. The following points are important to keep in mind when completing the measure:

- If the individual decides the domain is *not* important to them (i.e. if they assign a value 4 or less for importance), skip part b and do NOT rate time spent for that domain.

- The importance of the domain (e.g. education) should be rated according to their own *personal sense of importance*, rather than how much they believe the domain is valued by others or society generally. For example, while someone may think education is important *generally* (e.g. they may consider it important for their children), they may *not consider it as important* personally *for themselves*. For people with communication impairments, ensure they understand this concept through gestural or pictorial supports. For example, *'I want to know how important it is for you [point to the person, emphasise the word 'you']. Not for everyone else/ in general [point to yourself, and gesture to others outside], just you [point to person again].'*

- When rating the importance of the domain, it should be noted the measure is asking about the importance of the domain at the moment, rather than over the course of their life generally, how that domain was valued at some point in their past, or how it might be valued in future.

Note: a domain may still be important to the person even if they do not feel it applies to them at the moment. For example, if the individual is not a parent or not working at the moment, their values around parenting or work may still currently be important to them. The fact they are not able to engage in actions consistent with this value will be reflected in part b, as they will not be spending the time or effort they ideally would like to.

- To clarify this for people with communication impairments, you can rephrase 'at the moment' to *'right **now** in your life [gesture to the table indicating here and now]'.* You may need to repeat that phrase several times in your administration until you have a sense that the person understands that requirement.

- With the instruction *In the last week, how much quality time or effort have you spent on family? An ideal amount? Or not ideal?* you can enhance the communicative accessibility by pairing the words 'ideal amount' with a thumbs-up gesture, smile and head nod, or 'not ideal' with a thumbs-down, frown and shake of the head.

- When rating time spent on a domain (part b) it is important to rate how time or effort has been spent over the *last seven days*. Where the individual has not had a typical week in terms of their activities (e.g. they have been on holiday or in hospital), encourage them to rate domains in part b according to the last seven days, regardless of their usual routine.

- For people with communication impairments, ensure you point to the calendar and words showing 'in the past week' to reinforce this concept when the person is responding to the question. Again, this repetition may be required only for the first items and then could be withdrawn.

- Where there is cross-over between domains, a single action or activity can contribute towards multiple domains. For example, while 'volunteering' is provided as an example of participating in the community, some individuals may engage in volunteering as a way to prepare for returning to work after an injury. In this case, if it is relevant to the individual and they have spoken of volunteering, it may be considered when completing part b for both 'Community' and 'Work'.

- The examples included in part b for each domain are just some examples that may apply to that domain, but they are not exhaustive. If the individual has mentioned other activities which fall within a particular domain, it is permissible to verbally provide an example that may be relevant to the individual – for example, reminding them of their volunteering for the 'Work' domain. If an individual appears to be focused on the examples as the only options to comment on, remind the person *These are just examples to help you think. It could be the other things that you have talked about such as X [gesture where appropriate].*

THE WAY TO VALUED LIVING

goals and actions

Go for a 30-minute walk on Tues, Thurs and Sat

Eat fresh vegetables with dinner every day

Research and plan one new healthy meal

What can I do to help me achieve my goals?

Write a shopping list to remember ingredients

Use mindfulness to recognise the passengers

WRONG WAY GO BACK

THIS WAY

MY VALUE

To maintain a healthy lifestyle

Barriers:
- Not feeling motivated
- Forgetting to buy ingredients at the shops

References

Arch, J. J. & Craske, M. G. (2008). Acceptance and commitment therapy and cognitive behavioral therapy for anxiety disorders: Different treatments, similar mechanisms? *Clinical Psychology: Science and Practice*, 15(4), 263–279. https://doi.org/https://doi.org/10.1111/j.1468-2850.2008.00137.x

Barney, J. L., Lillis, J., Haynos, A. F., Forman, E. & Juarascio, A. S. (2019). Assessing the valuing process in Acceptance and Commitment Therapy: Experts' review of the current status and recommendations for future measure development. *Journal of Contextual Behavioral Science*, 12, 225–233. https://doi.org/https://doi.org/10.1016/j.jcbs.2018.08.002

Baseotto, M. C., Morris, P. G., Gillespie, D. C. & Trevethan, C. T. (2022). Post-traumatic growth and value-directed living after acquired brain injury. *Neuropsychological Rehabilitation*, 32(1), 84–103. https://doi.org/10.1080/09602011.2020.1798254

Draper, K., Ponsford, J. & Schönberger, M. (2007). Psychosocial and emotional outcomes 10 years following traumatic brain injury. *Journal of Head Trauma Rehabilitation*, 22(5), 278–287. https://doi.org/10.1097/01.HTR.0000290972.63753.a7

Emery, H., Padgett, C., Ownsworth, T. & Honan, C. A. (2022). A systematic review of self-concept change in multiple sclerosis. *Neuropsychological Rehabilitation*, 32(8), 1774–1813. https://doi.org/10.1080/09602011.2022.2030367

Fadyl, J. K., Theadom, A., Channon, A. & McPherson, K. M. (2019). Recovery and adaptation after traumatic brain injury in New Zealand: Longitudinal qualitative findings over the first two years. *Neuropsychological Rehabilitation*, 29(7), 1095–1112. https://doi.org/10.1080/09602011.2017.1364653

Fejo-King, C. (2013). *Let's talk kinship: innovating Australian social work education, theory, research and practice through Aboriginal knowledge: Insights from social work research conducted with the Larrakia and Warumungu Peoples of the Northern Territory*. Christine Fejo-King Consulting.

Fraas, M. R. & Calvert, M. (2009). The use of narratives to identify characteristics leading to a productive life following acquired brain injury. *American Journal of Speech-Language Pathology*, 18(4), 315–328. https://doi.org/10.1044/1058-0360(2009/08-0008)

Gracey, F., Evans, J. J. & Malley, D. (2009). Capturing process and outcome in complex rehabilitation interventions: A 'Y-shaped' model. *Neuropsychological Rehabilitation*, 19(6), 867–890. https://doi.org/10.1080/09602010903027763

Hanel, P. H. P., Maio, G. R., Soares, A. K. S., Vione, K. C. *et al.* (2018). Cross-cultural differences and similarities in human value instantiation. *Frontiers in Psychology*, 9. https://doi.org/10.3389/fpsyg.2018.00849

Hayes, S. C., Luoma, J. B., Bond, F. W., Masuda, A. & Lillis, J. (2006). Acceptance and commitment therapy: Model, processes and outcomes. *Behaviour Research and Therapy*, 44(1), 1–25. https://doi.org/10.1016/j.brat.2005.06.006

Hayes, S. C., Strosahl, K. D. & Wilson, K. G. (2012). *Acceptance and Commitment Therapy: The Process and Practice of Mindful Change* (2nd edition). New York, NY: Guilford Press.

Jumisko, E., Lexell, J. & Söderberg, S. (2005). The meaning of living with traumatic brain injury in people with moderate or severe traumatic brain injury. *Journal of Neuroscience Nursing*, 37(1), 42–50. https://doi.org/10.1097/01376517-200502000-00007

King, L. A. & Hicks, J. A. (2021). The science of meaning in life. *Annual Review of Psychology*, 72, 561–584. https://doi.org/10.1146/annurev-psych-072420-122921

Lennon, A., Bramham, J., Carroll, À., McElligott, J. *et al.* (2014). A qualitative exploration of how individuals reconstruct their sense of self following acquired brain injury

in comparison with spinal cord injury. *Brain Injury*, 28(1), 27–37. https://doi.org/1
0.3109/02699052.2013.848378

Lundgren, T., Luoma, J. B., Dahl, J., Strosahl, K. & Melin, L. (2012). The Bull's-Eye Values
Survey: A psychometric evaluation. *Cognitive and Behavioral Practice*, 19(4), 518–526.
https://doi.org/https://doi.org/10.1016/j.cbpra.2012.01.004

Majumdar, S. & Morris, R. (2019). Brief group-based acceptance and commitment therapy for stroke survivors. *British Journal of Clinical Psychology*, 58(1), 70–90. https://
doi.org/10.1111/bjc.12198

McCracken, L. M. & Yang, S.-Y. (2006). The role of values in a contextual cognitive-be-
havioral approach to chronic pain. *Pain*, 123, 137–145. https://doi.org/10.1016/j.
pain.2006.02.021

McGrath, J. (2004). Beyond restoration to transformation: Positive outcomes in the
rehabilitation of acquired brain injury. *Clinical Rehabilitation*, 18(7), 767–775.
https://doi.org/10.1191/0269215504cr802oa

Michelson, S. E., Lee, J. K., Orsillo, S. M. & Roemer, L. (2011). The role of values-consis-
tent behavior in generalized anxiety disorder. *Depression and Anxiety*, 28(5), 358–366.
https://doi.org/10.1002/da.20793

Miller, H., Lawson, D., Power, E., das Nair, R., Sathananthan, N. & Wong, D. (2022). How
do people with acquired brain injury interpret the Valued Living Questionnaire? A
cognitive interviewing study. *Journal of Contextual Behavioral Science*, 23, 125–136.
https://doi.org/https://doi.org/10.1016/j.jcbs.2022.01.003

Mulahalilović, A., Hasanović, M., Pajević, I. & Jakovljević, M. (2021). Meaning and the
sense of meaning in life from a health perspective. *Psychiatria Danubina*, 33(4),
1025–1031.

Pais, C., Ponsford, J. L., Gould, K. R. & Wong, D. (2019). Role of valued living and associations with functional outcome following traumatic brain injury. *Neuropsychological
Rehabilitation*, 29(4), 625–637. https://doi.org/10.1080/09602011.2017.1313745

Pais-Hrit, C., Wong, D., Gould, K. R. & Ponsford, J. (2020). Behavioural and functional
correlates of post-traumatic growth following traumatic brain injury. *Neuropsychological Rehabilitation*, 30(7), 1205–1223. https://doi.org/10.1080/09602011.2019.
1569536

Rose, A. & Rendell, L. (2022). A values-based approach to goal setting in neuro-rehabilitation following severe brain injury: An audit of service development. *The
Neuropsychologist*, 1(14), 37–46.

Sander, A. M., Clark, A. N., Arciniegas, D. B., Tran, K. *et al.* (2021). A randomized controlled trial of acceptance and commitment therapy for psychological distress
among persons with traumatic brain injury. *Neuropsychological Rehabilitation*, 31(7),
1105–1129. https://doi.org/10.1080/09602011.2020.1762670

Sathananthan, N., Dimech-Betancourt, B., Morris, E., Vicendese, D. *et al.* (2021). A single-case experimental evaluation of a new group-based intervention to enhance
adjustment to life with acquired brain injury: VaLiANT (Valued Living After Neurological Trauma). *Neuropsychological Rehabilitation*, 32(8), 2170–2202. https://doi.
org/10.1080/09602011.2021.1971094

Sathananthan, N., Morris, E. M. J., Gillanders, D., Knox, L. *et al.* (2022). Does integrating
cognitive and psychological interventions enhance wellbeing after acquired brain
injury? Study protocol for a Phase II randomized controlled trial of the VaLiANT
(Valued Living After Neurological Trauma) Group Program. *Frontiers in Rehabilitation Sciences*, 2. https://doi.org/10.3389/fresc.2021.815111

Sathananthan, N., Morris, E., Gillanders, D., das Nair, R., Knox, L., & Wong, D. (2024). Rebuilding the self through valued action and group connections after ABI: participant perspectives on the VaLiANT group intervention. *Neuropsychological rehabilitation, 35*(4), 728–756.

Scobbie, L., Thomson, K., Pollock, A. & Evans, J. (2021). Goal adjustment by people living with long-term conditions: A scoping review of literature published from January 2007 to June 2018. *Neuropsychological Rehabilitation, 31*(8), 1314–1345. https://doi.org/10.1080/09602011.2020.1774397

Sheppard, S. C., Forsyth, J. P., Hickling, E. J. & Bianchi, J. (2010). A novel application of acceptance and commitment therapy for psychosocial problems associated with multiple sclerosis: Results from a half-day workshop intervention. *International Journal of MS Care, 12*(4), 200–206. https://doi.org/https://doi.org/10.7224/1537-2073-12.4.200

Shipley, J., Luker, J., Thijs, V. & Bernhardt, J. (2018). The personal and social experiences of community-dwelling younger adults after stroke in Australia: A qualitative interview study. *BMJ Open, 8*(12), e023525. https://doi.org/10.1136/bmjopen-2018-023525

Skaliotis, J., Miller, H., & Wong, D. (2025). Validation of the valued living questionnaire - comprehension support version (VLQ-CS) in a neurotypical adult cohort. *The behaviour therapist.*

Smout, M., Davies, M., Burns, N. & Christie, A. (2014). Development of the Valuing Questionnaire (VQ). *Journal of Contextual Behavioral Science, 3*(3), 164–172. https://doi.org/10.1016/j.jcbs.2014.06.001

Stolwyk, R. J., Mihaljcic, T., Wong, D. K., Chapman, J. E. & Rogers, J. M. (2021). Poststroke cognitive impairment negatively impacts activity and participation outcomes: A systematic review and meta-analysis. *Stroke, 52*(2), 748–760. https://doi.org/10.1161/strokeaha.120.032215

Theadom, A., Starkey, N., Barker-Collo, S., Jones, K. *et al.* (2018). Population-based cohort study of the impacts of mild traumatic brain injury in adults four years post-injury. *PLoS One, 13*(1), e0191655. https://doi.org/10.1371/journal.pone.0191655

Vaghela, R., Santoro, C. & Braham, L. (2021). The psychological adjustment needs of individuals following an acquired brain injury: A systematic review. *Applied Neuropsychology: Adult,* 1–14. https://doi.org/10.1080/23279095.2021.1956927

Van Bost, G., Van Damme, S. & Crombez, G. (2020). Goal reengagement is related to mental well-being, life satisfaction and acceptance in people with an acquired brain injury. *Neuropsychological Rehabilitation, 30*(9), 1814–1828. https://doi.org/10.1080/09602011.2019.1608265

Whiting, D. L., Deane, F., McLeod, H., Ciarrochi, J. & Simpson, G. (2020). Can acceptance and commitment therapy facilitate psychological adjustment after a severe traumatic brain injury? A pilot randomized controlled trial. *Neuropsychological Rehabilitation, 30*(7), 1348–1371. https://doi.org/10.1080/09602011.2019.1583582

Wilson, K. G., Sandoz, E. K., Kitchens, J. & Roberts, M. (2010). The Valued Living Questionnaire: Defining and measuring valued action within a behavioral framework. *The Psychological Record, 60*(2), 249–272. https://doi.org/10.1007/BF03395706

Wong, D., Hsieh, M-Y., McKay, A. J. D., Haines, K., O'Donnell, M. & Ponsford, J. L. (2019). *Cognitive Behaviour Therapy for anxiety and depression – Adapted for Brain Injury (CBT-ABI): A Treatment Manual.* Australasian Society for the Study of Brain Impairment.

Wong, D., Miller, H., Lawson, D., Borschmann, K. *et al.* (under review). *Development and validation of the Valued Living Questionnaire – Comprehension Support Version (VLQ-CS).*

CHAPTER 7

Committed Action

REBECCA GOULD

Luke: 'Alright, I'll give it a try.'
Yoda: 'No, try not. Do or do not. There is no try.'

STAR WARS EPISODE V: THE EMPIRE STRIKES BACK

About the author

Rebecca Gould, PhD, DClinPsy, is a Professor of Psychological Therapies in the Division of Psychiatry at University College London and an Honorary Clinical Psychologist in Camden and Islington NHS Foundation Trust. Her main research interests are in developing and evaluating psychological interventions, particularly third-wave therapies such as ACT and mindfulness-based interventions, for people living with physical and mental health conditions. With respect to neurological conditions, she is currently leading a clinical trial examining the clinical and cost-effectiveness of ACT for improving psychological health in comparison to multidisciplinary usual care for people living with motor neurone disease. She is also currently developing an intervention based on ACT for people affected by Parkinson's disease, as well as being a co-applicant in a clinical trial examining ACT for caregivers of people living with dementia. She mostly draws on ACT and mindfulness-based approaches in her clinical and professional practice.

What is committed action?

Committed action is one of the six core processes in the hexaflex that is used to develop psychological flexibility (Hayes, Strosahl & Wilson, 2012). It refers to committing to engaging in personally meaningful, life-enriching activities or choosing to act in ways that are consistent with one's values, alongside one's internal experiences (e.g. thoughts, images, memories, emotions, sensations or urges). It involves building larger and larger patterns of action that support effective values-based living and uses a combination of motivation and behaviour change processes to facilitate meaningful behavioural change.

The psychologically inflexible counterpart of committed action is inaction, impulsivity or avoidant persistence. Inaction is seen when there is a failure to take action in service of one's chosen values. Impulsivity refers to engaging in impulsive or self-defeating behaviours such as substance use or engaging in risky or self-injurious behaviour. Avoidant persistence means persisting in engaging in experiential avoidance, even when this is no longer workable. These indicators of psychological inflexibility are of particular importance where neurological conditions are concerned since they may overlap with cognitive impairment (e.g. deficits in executive functioning such as reduced initiation, perseveration, impulsivity and disinhibition). Furthermore, other external factors such as physical health or mobility issues may serve as barriers to committed action. Consequently, incorporating ways to overcome external barriers such as these within committed action is a key adaptation for people living with neurological conditions that is explored further in this chapter.

Key principles in committed action
Effective goal setting

Effective goal setting in ACT involves a number of key steps. The first step is to choose a high priority valued direction. This is useful within the context of neurological conditions given that people may have limited energy and resources to focus on their valued directions. The next step is to develop an action plan for values-based behavioural change using traditional goal-setting principles. That is, to develop SMART goals (i.e. goals that are Specific, Measurable, Attainable, Relevant and Time-specific) that will help move a person in the direction of their high priority value. After this, these values-based SMART goals should be broken down into specific actions or smaller, more manageable steps that can be achieved in the next day(s), week(s), month(s) and year. A crucial part of effective goal setting within the context of neurological conditions is the fourth step: identifying any external barriers to actions (e.g. physical health, mobility or cognitive difficulties) and ways of overcoming them. Strategies for overcoming such barriers using principles of selection, optimisation and compensation are explored later in this chapter. Distressing or unwanted internal experiences (e.g. thoughts, images, memories, emotion, sensations and urges) may serve as additional barriers to actions. Consequently, the fifth step involves identifying these internal barriers, as well as ways of overcoming them using acceptance, defusion and mindfulness skills (as explored in other chapters). The final step involves helping a person to commit to goals and actions that are set in service of their values using motivational and behavioural reinforcement strategies. For example, the person can be encouraged to make a public commitment by publicising their goal/action plan (e.g. by telling their partner, family or friend about it). Once these steps have been completed, a person is encouraged to broaden their behavioural repertoires by repeating these cyclical steps with larger patterns of values-based action or extending them to other domains.

Setting ACT-consistent goals

It is important to remember that the aim of ACT is not to reduce distress or symptoms, though this can happen as a 'by-product' of people living their lives in personally meaningful ways, alongside their distressing or unwanted experiences. Consequently, goals need to be set that are consistent with this aim. Harris (2009) describes three types of goals that can act as potential pitfalls when developing committed action: emotional goals, dead person's goals and insight goals. Emotional goals (e.g. 'I want to feel better' or 'I want to feel calmer') are goals in which the aim is to feel a certain way. Dead person's goals (e.g. 'I want to stop feeling angry' or 'I want to stop arguing with my partner') are goals that a dead person can do better than a live human being, as a corpse can never feel angry or argue with somebody. The aim of these types of goals is to stop feeling or behaving in a certain way. Insight goals (e.g. 'I want to know why this has happened to me' or 'I want to know why I am the way I am') are goals where the aim is to gain a greater understanding of oneself and, in the process, feel better about oneself.

Although these types of goals are completely natural and understandable, particularly within the context of acquired neurological conditions, they need to be reframed into ACT-consistent goals, otherwise experiential avoidance or emotional control will be positively reinforced. Harris (2009) suggests that there are a number of ways in which these types of goals can be reframed into ACT-consistent goals, as shown in Table 7.1.

Table 7.1: How to reframe emotional goals, dead person's goals and insight goals

ACT-inconsistent goal	How to elicit an ACT-consistent goal
Emotional goal (e.g. 'I want to feel better', 'I want to feel calmer')	Suppose you were feeling better/calmer, what would you be doing differently? What would you be doing that you're not doing now?
	Suppose I waved a magic wand and all these distressing thoughts and feelings were no longer having an impact on you.* What would you be doing differently?
Dead person's goal (e.g. 'I want to stop feeling angry', 'I want to stop arguing with my partner')	If you weren't feeling angry, what would you be doing differently? If I were a fly on the wall, what would I see?
	If you weren't arguing with your partner, how would you be interacting with them?
Insight goal (e.g. 'I want to know why this has happened to me', 'I want to know why I am the way I am')	If you were to gain that insight and understanding about why this has happened to you, what would you be doing differently?

* In this example, it is important to emphasise 'thoughts and feelings were no longer having an impact on you' rather than 'thoughts and feelings disappeared' as the latter is not consistent with the aim of ACT.

Positively reinforcing behavioural change

Given that ACT is typically focused on shifting a person from the notion of 'short-term gain creating long-term pain' to 'short-term pain creating long-term gain' when what they're doing is no longer workable, it is important that we find ways to make unwanted internal experiences appetitive rather than aversive. One way we can do this is by positively reinforcing any actions or smaller steps taken in service of values. Some suggestions as to how this can be achieved are outlined in Table 7.2. If memory impairment interferes with recall of the positive consequences or benefits of action then positively reinforcing this through present moment awareness is crucial.

Table 7.2: How to positively reinforce any action taken in service of values

Component of positive reinforcement	Example
Notice what was in their experience when they completed the action	What did you notice when you did X? How did you feel? What thoughts went through your mind? And what about now as we talk about it?
Notice the positive or desirable consequences of the behaviour	What happened after you did X? And then what? What were the benefits of doing X?
Notice the choices they had in this situation	What choices did you have in this situation? What else could you have chosen to do? Can we just notice that you could have chosen to do Y but you chose to do X? You chose to experience the distressing thoughts, feelings and sensations in order that you could do something or act in a way that was important to you. What did you get by being willing to experience the distressing thoughts, feelings and sensations?
Notice the values underlying the behaviour	Why was it important for you to do X? You could have done Y but you did X – what was important about that to you?
Notice whether it moved them towards or away from the things that are important and matter to them	How did it help you to do what you want to do in the way that you want to do it? Was this a move towards or away from the things that are important and matter to you?

Measuring engaged living

Numerous measures can be used to assess the extent to which a person is living their life in accordance with their values. However, few have been validated in people living with neurological conditions. Foote *et al.* (2022) conducted a scoping review of measures relevant to ACT processes that have been used in adults with acquired neurological conditions such as multiple sclerosis (MS), dementia, traumatic brain injury (TBI) and stroke. The review identified 54 studies, but only identified three that had included a tool which the reviewing authors suggested could be used to assess committed action. Two studies used the Motivation for Traumatic Brain Injury Rehabilitation Questionnaire (MOT-Q) (Chervinsky *et al.*, 1998), a 31-item questionnaire that examines motivation for and attitudes towards post-acute rehabilitation in TBI. It is important to note that the MOT-Q was not developed specifically with ACT in mind and is therefore limited in its ability to capture key components of engaged living (such as linking values to committed action).

One study reported including the Engaged Living Scale (ELS) (Trompetter *et al.*, 2013) in a clinical trial protocol of ACT for people living with TBI (Whiting *et al.*, 2021). The ELS is a 16-item scale that was developed specifically to assess an engaged response style in ACT (i.e. the extent to which a person knows what matters to them and takes action to do what matters to them). It was originally validated in people with chronic pain and was found to have good internal reliability. It has since been validated in people living with acquired brain injury (Baseotto *et al.*, 2022), and so is recommended here for assessing committed action in people living with TBI. Further research is needed before it can be recommended for use in other neurological conditions. An alternative to the ELS is the use of two subscales on committed action and 'inaction' from the Multidimensional Psychological Flexibility Inventory (MPFI) (Rolffs, Rogge & Wilson, 2018), which has been validated in people living with MS (Giovannetti *et al.*, 2022).

Evidence for committed action

As McCracken (2021) notes, there is a vast amount of evidence for behavioural change processes such as goal setting (Epton, Currie & Armitage, 2017) and behavioural activation (Stein *et al.*, 2020). However, previous lab-based studies of the specific process of committed action, as defined within ACT and as an isolated ACT process, are lacking. This is most likely due to the overlap with previous studies of behavioural change processes and the interrelatedness of ACT core processes such as values, respectively. The interrelated nature of the core processes of committed action and values was demonstrated in a recent network analysis by Christodoulou *et al.* (2023). These authors conducted a network analysis of the Psychological Flexibility/Psychological Inflexibility model in two different sample groups, one of whom completed various questionnaires, including a measure of psychological flexibility, the Multidimensional Psychological Flexibility Inventory, and one of whom completed questionnaires assessing the six core ACT processes. Committed action and values emerged as a strongly associated and combined component of the Psychological Flexibility/Psychological Inflexibility model. This highlights the importance of committed action completed in service of values, as postulated within ACT, and distinguishes committed action from mere goal setting and behavioural activation.

Adaptations within the context of neurological conditions

Careful consideration needs to be given to committed action within the context of neurological conditions, since people may be faced with a multitude of internal and external barriers that may get in the way of this. Internal barriers to action include distressing or unwanted thoughts, images, memories, emotions, sensations and urges, whereas external barriers include symptoms or deficits relating to the neurological condition, as well as other contextual factors (e.g. social, financial, occupational, leisure and environmental issues). Some examples of these relevant to people living with neurological conditions are shown in Table 7.3. Previous chapters have explored how to effectively handle internal barriers so that they have less impact on a person's life through the use of acceptance, defusion and mindfulness skills. Ways of overcoming external barriers, alongside internal barriers, through the use of selection, optimisation and compensation principles will be explored next.

Table 7.3: Internal and external barriers to committed action relevant to neurological conditions

Internal barrier	Example
Thoughts	'Why me?', 'I'm a burden on others', 'I'm not the person I used to be'
Images	Images of how the neurological condition will progress in the future
Memories	Memories of how things used to be, memories of a previous family member
Emotions	Sadness, anger, guilt, worry and anxiety
Physical sensations	Breathlessness due to anxiety
External barrier	**Example**
Health-related issues	Symptoms or deficits in physical, cognitive or communicative functioning
Social issues	Lack of social support
Financial issues	Not having enough money
Occupational or leisure issues	Not having enough time, difficulties juggling appointments
Environmental issues	Not being able to access friends' homes due to using a wheelchair

Selection, optimisation and compensation principles were originally developed to aid adaptation to the challenges of ageing (Baltes, 1990). They involve strategies for maximising gains and minimising losses in order to promote successful ageing. Selection comprises prioritising and selecting goals in response to a reduction in resources such as losses in function due to physical or cognitive difficulties. This may be achieved in two ways: through elective selection which involves prioritising or selecting goals based on personal preferences, and through loss-based selection which involves abandoning goals due to losses in resources. Optimisation involves optimising goal-related activity through investment of resources and effort in order to maximise chances of achieving set goals. Finally, compensation refers to identifying ways to compensate for losses in resources such as through the use of external resources, aids and adaptations or seeking support from others.

These strategies have been applied to cognitive behavioural

therapy for older people (Chellingsworth, Kishita & Laidlaw, 2016) and ACT for older people with chronic pain (Alonso-Fernandez *et al.*, 2016), older people with treatment-resistant generalised anxiety disorder (Gould *et al.*, 2021), and people living with motor neurone disease (MND) (Gould *et al.*, 2022, 2023). They can be similarly applied to people living with other neurological conditions to help them achieve values-based goals despite the challenges or losses presented by their conditions. As an example, Table 7.4 illustrates how these strategies can be applied to a person living with MND.

Table 7.4: Applying selection, optimisation and compensation principles to ACT for people with neurological conditions

Case example: Priya is a professional artist who was diagnosed with MND four years ago. MND is a fatal neurodegenerative disease that affects motor neurons from the motor cortex to the spinal cord, and causes progressive wasting and weakness in muscles involved in movement, speaking, swallowing and breathing. She is no longer able to paint with her hands due to limited physical mobility, but she is able to move her eyes. She has recently learned how to use an eye tracker on her laptop to communicate with others.

Strategy	What it involves	How it can be applied to ACT	Example
Selection	Prioritising and selecting goals in response to a reduction in resources – choosing what to focus one's remaining resources on.	Select or limit personally meaningful goals to those that are in service of the person's most important values at this point in their life.	Priya used the Life Compass exercise to identify her most important value (acting with creativity). She selected a goal of creating artwork in service of acting with creativity.
		Select or limit personally meaningful goals to those that are in the best domains of physical or mental functioning.	She selected goals in relation to eye movements as she was still able to do this.
		Adapt personally meaningful goals or focus on specific aspects of a goal so that they can be more realistically achieved.	She adapted her goal of creating artwork so that it incorporated the use of an eye tracker on her laptop as she was already familiar with this.
		Replace personally meaningful goals that are no longer achievable by identifying the underlying value and exploring different ways in which that value can be met.	She recognised that she was no longer able to create artwork using her hands, but could still act with creativity in other ways (e.g. by creating digital artwork through eye movements).

Strategy	What it involves	How it can be applied to ACT	Example
Optimisation	Investing resources and effort in order to maximise chances of achieving set goals.	Optimise engagement in goal-related activities by engaging in training or acquiring new knowledge and skills.	She learnt how to create digital artwork using an eye tracker and art software.
		Optimise engagement in goal-related activities by practising new or previously learned skills.	She repeatedly practised creating digital artwork using an eye tracker and art software.
		Optimise engagement in goal-related activities by capitalising on a person's strengths.	She maximised her chances of creating digital artwork using an eye tracker and art software by putting her new skills with assistive technology to use.
Compensation	Identifying ways to compensate for losses in resources.	Utilise additional resources so that personally meaningful goals can be achieved (e.g. by seeking support from others).	She asked her partner for help with setting up the art software on her PC and integrating the eye tracker with it.
		Use alternative aids, adaptations or tools to compensate for losses in physical or mental functioning.	She used an eye tracker and art software on her PC to compensate for losses in physical functioning.
		Use alternative strategies (e.g. mnemonic strategies) to compensate for losses in physical or mental functioning.	She recognised that learning new skills was tiring for her and so used a variety of strategies to manage her fatigue (e.g. pacing herself, using the software at the best times of day for her, restricting activity to 20–30 minutes and then resting).

Useful metaphors and experiential exercises for developing committed action

Travel itinerary metaphor

Developing committed action involves planning or choosing what one will do in service of one's values, doing what one has planned and persisting in doing what one has planned or changing this, where necessary. Hence, a useful metaphor to consider when developing committed action is the travel itinerary metaphor, which is an extension of the compass metaphor that is frequently used when examining values. In the travel itinerary metaphor, valued life directions are the compass headings for the journey, whereas goals and actions are the stops along the journey or the signposts that let you know you are headed in the right direction and are keeping on track. Failure to carry out planned actions due to inaction or avoidance can be viewed as detours on the journey: an opportunity to notice the internal barriers that got in the way of action, renew the commitment and get back on track.

Of particular relevance to people living with neurological conditions, external barriers such as cognitive, physical health, social, financial, occupational, leisure or environmental issues (see Table 7.3) can be viewed as road blocks that limit the roads one can take on this journey. These can be handled by either waiting for the block to be cleared or finding another route around them. As the natural response when faced with external barriers is to give up rather than find another route, it is important to help people notice the internal barriers that show up in response to these external barriers. For example, thoughts such as 'What's the point?' and 'It's not the same', emotions such as frustration and sadness, and sensations such as agitation. Following this, the use of acceptance, defusion and mindfulness skills to unhook or step back from such internal experiences should be explored further.

As noted earlier in this chapter, it may be difficult at times to differentiate between a lack of committed action (i.e. inaction, impulsivity or avoidant persistence) and interference from external barriers (e.g. deficits in executive functioning such as reduced initiation, perseveration, impulsivity and disinhibition). Bringing present moment awareness to barriers that are serving as obstacles to committed action is crucial for disentangling external barriers from internal barriers.

Small Steps exercise

A useful way of helping people to notice the internal barriers that show up as soon as they start to consider making progress in their lives in ways that are important and meaningful to them is the Small Steps exercise (Scott *et al.*, 2018). This involves inviting a person to bring one of their values to mind and to consider actions or steps they could take that would help them move in this valued direction over the next six months or so, then the next month, next week and next day. The person is encouraged to notice the thoughts, images, memories, sensations and urges that show up as they consider these actions or steps, and to notice how they are reacting to these internal experiences. This can then be used as an opportunity to explore the workability of what the person does when these internal experiences are around, and to practise acceptance, defusion and mindfulness skills to unhook or step back from them.

An example script for the Small Steps exercise is presented in Appendix 7.1 at the end of this chapter. A much briefer version of the Small Steps exercise involves simply asking a person 'What's the smallest step you could take that would move you towards one of your values in the next week? Now would you be willing to take this smallest step?' If the person says no then present moment awareness can be used to identify the internal barriers to action (e.g. 'As we talk about this right now, what are you noticing? What is your mind telling you? What feelings are here? What are you noticing in your body?').

Goals, Actions and Values Plan

The Goals, Actions and Values Plan (Appendix 7.2), incorporating selection, optimisation and compensation strategies, is a useful exercise for accounting for both internal and external barriers faced by people living with neurological conditions. It involves identifying a person's goal, as well as the underlying value, and the external barriers that might get in the way of this. If external barriers are present then it involves identifying selection, optimisation and compensation strategies that can be used to overcome the external barriers. It is then about breaking down the goal into smaller actions or steps, and finally considering any internal barriers or additional external barriers that might interfere with successful completion of these actions, as well as ways to overcome them. Encouraging people to identify small steps in service of values in the Goals, Actions and Values Plan and then to 'go even smaller' can be a helpful way of ensuring 'easy wins' and building motivation through positive reinforcement.

An illustration of how the Goals, Actions and Values Plan can be used with people living with neurological conditions is presented in the following case example: Joseph is 34 years old and was diagnosed with MND eight months ago. He is still working as a computer technician, and lives with his partner and daughter, Lucy, who is six years old. The main symptoms of MND that are troubling him at present include a weak voice and fatigue. As shown in Table 7.5, Joseph and his therapist worked together to create a Goals, Actions and Values Plan that would help him to make progress in his life in important and meaningful ways, while compensating for physical and communicative difficulties caused by MND.

Other experiential exercises and metaphors for developing committed action

Many other experiential exercises and metaphors exist for developing committed action in ACT, and listing these here is beyond the scope of this chapter. For example, Stoddard and Afari (2014) provide numerous examples that could be potentially used with people living with neurological conditions. The key thing to ensure is that any experiential exercises or metaphors are adapted so that they are matched to an individual's psychological, physical, cognitive and communicative needs.

Table 7.5: Joseph's Goals, Actions and Values Plan incorporating selection, optimisation and compensation strategies

1. What do I want to do? What is my goal?

Read bedtime stories to Lucy.

2. Why is this goal important to me? What type of person do I want to be alongside the difficulties I am experiencing? How do I want to be acting or behaving?

I want to be a loving and caring dad.

3. What difficulties with my health, financial, occupational, leisure or social situation get in the way of my goal?

My voice is weak and I get tired easily because of MND.

4. How can I best focus my energy and resources on my goal? Select all that apply.

☒ Choose a goal that connects with a value that is the most important to me.

☐ Choose a goal that is in my best area of functioning.

☐ Adapt the goal so that it can be more realistically achieved.

☐ Replace the goal with another goal that can be more realistically achieved.

Further details:

Being a loving and caring dad is in the top three most important values for me.

5. How can I optimise or increase my chances of achieving my goal? Select all that apply.

☐ Learn a new skill.

☐ Practise a skill.

☒ Capitalise on what I can do or what I'm good at.

Further details:

I can still talk, even though my voice is weak.

6. How can I compensate for difficulties with my health, financial, occupational, leisure or social situation in order that I can achieve my goal? Select all that apply.

☐ Seek support from elsewhere.

☐ Ask for help from others.

☒ Use equipment, aids or tools.

☒ Use physical or cognitive strategies to compensate for my difficulties.

Further details:

I could use a microphone or voice amplifier to compensate for my voice being weak.

As my voice will become weaker in the future, I could consider voice banking.

I could also record me reading some of Lucy's favourite bedtime stories.

To compensate for getting tired easily, I could just read four or five pages at a time rather than the whole chapter.

I could also encourage Lucy to share the reading with me (e.g. she reads one sentence and I read the next).

7. What are the smallest actions or steps I can take to achieve my goal?

Goal: Read bedtime stories to Lucy.

Step 1:
- What? Have a look at microphones and voice amplifiers on Amazon.
- When by? 14 September

Step 2:
- What? Buy a microphone or voice amplifier.
- When by? 16 September

Step 3:
- What? Ask Lucy what her favourite bedtime stories are.
- When by? 18 September

Step 4:
- What? Have a look at voice banking on the MND Association's website.
- When by? 25 September

Step 5:
- What? Record me reading some of Lucy's favourite bedtime stories.
- When by? 16 October

8. What potential barriers might get in the way of me achieving my goal? Potential barriers include:

- Financial, social, occupational or leisure barriers (e.g. not having enough time or money, lack of social support)
- Health-related barriers (e.g. difficulties with mobility, communication, memory problems, fatigue)
- Private or internal barriers (e.g. thoughts, feelings, images, memories, bodily sensations, urges)

How can I handle these potential barriers so that I can achieve my goal?

List each potential barrier	List ways of handling each potential barrier
Not having enough time or forgetting to complete the steps.	Schedule times in the diary to complete each step.
Weak voice.	Use a microphone or voice amplifier.
Feeling too tired.	Don't try and do all the steps at once – pace myself and break them down into even smaller steps, if necessary.
Thoughts such as 'I'm weak and useless' and 'What's the point? Lucy won't want to hear my weak voice'.	Practise stepping back from this thought using the 'I notice I'm having...' exercise.
Feeling sad and overwhelmed as soon as I start to try and complete any of the goals.	Practise being willing to have these difficult feelings in order that I can be the loving and caring dad that I want to be – remember the ticket metaphor!
Images of me not being able to talk and not being around for Lucy in the future.	Practise coming back to the present moment rather than getting caught up in images of the future.

Considerations when working with families and healthcare professionals

The main considerations when working with families and healthcare professionals are threefold. First, it should be ensured that family members (in addition to the person with a neurological condition) are on board with the aims of ACT – an issue that is relevant to all preceding chapters and not just this one. Second, it is important to check that goals set in the Goals, Actions and Values Plan are realistic and achievable given that they may require input from other family members, depending on the degree to which the neurological condition impacts daily functioning. Inviting family members to join sessions in which the Goals, Actions and Values Plan is discussed, with the consent of the person with a neurological condition, can be beneficial in ensuring this. Third, it is important to ensure that the Goals, Actions and Values Plan is meaningful to the person with a neurological condition, rather than potentially reflecting the family's or healthcare professional's goals. Clarifying the person's values underlying any goals set and being on the lookout for pliance (and addressing this, if necessary) will ensure that the Goals, Actions and Values Plan is meaningful to the person with a neurological condition.

Summary

In summary, this chapter has explored one of the six core processes in the hexaflex, committed action, and how this can be adapted for people living with neurological conditions. It has considered the key principles that apply to committed action, how external and internal barriers to committed action that are relevant to neurological conditions can be addressed, and useful experiential exercises and metaphors that can be considered when developing committed action in people living with neurological conditions.

As Hayes *et al.* (2012, p.328) stated, 'if a client does not change his or her behaviour, then all of our efforts working on defusion-acceptance, present moment-self-as-perspective, and values are for naught'. It is hoped that this chapter has provided useful guidance as to how to help a person living with neurological conditions to change their behaviour in values-based ways, thus ensuring that these efforts are not for naught.

References

Alonso-Fernandez, M. A., Lopez-Lopez, A., Losada, A., Gonzalez, J. L. & Loebach Wetherell, J. (2016). Acceptance and commitment therapy and selective optimization with compensation for institutionalised older people with chronic pain. *Pain Medicine*, 17(2), 264–277.

Baltes, P. B. (1990). Psychological Perspectives on Successful Aging: The Model of Selective Optimization with Compensation. In P. B. Baltes & M. M. Baltes (eds), *Successful Aging: Perspectives from the Behavioral Sciences* (pp.1–34). Cambridge, UK: Cambridge University Press.

Baseotto, M. C., Morris, P. G., Gillespie, D. C. & Trevethan, C. T. (2022). Post-traumatic growth and value-directed living after acquired brain injury. *Neuropsychological Rehabilitation*, 32(1), 84–103.

Chellingsworth, M., Kishita, N. & Laidlaw, K. (2016). *A Clinician's Guide to Low Intensity CBT with Older People.* Available at: https://issuu.com/ueadeparmentofclinpsychcbt/docs/final_licbt_with_older_people.

Chervinsky, A. B., Ommaya, A. K., deJonge, M., Spector, J., Schwab, K. & Salazar, A. M. (1998). Motivation for traumatic brain injury rehabilitation questionnaire (MOT-Q): Reliability, factor analysis, and relationship to MMPI-2 variables. *Archives of Clinical Neuropsychology*, 13, 433–446.

Christodoulou, A., Karekla, M., Costantini, G. & Michaelides, M. P. (2023). A network analysis approach on the Psychological Flexibility/Inflexibility model. *Behavior Therapy*, 54(5), 719–733.

Epton, T., Currie, S. & Armitage, C. J. (2017). Unique effects of setting goals on behavior change: Systemic review and meta-analysis. *Journal of Consulting and Clinical Psychology*, 85(12), 1182–1198.

Foote, H., Bowen, A., Cotterill, S., Hill, G., Pieri, M. & Patchwood, E. (2022). A scoping review to identify process and outcome measures used in acceptance and commitment therapy research, with adults with acquired neurological conditions. *Clinical Rehabilitation*, 37(6), 808–835.

Giovannetti, A. M., Pakenham, K. I., Presti, G. *et al.* (2022). A group resilience training program for people with multiple sclerosis: Study protocol of a multi-centre cluster-randomized controlled trial (multi-READY for MS). *PLoS One*, 17(5), e0267245.

Gould, R. L., Loebach Wetherell, J., Kimona, K., Serfaty, M. A. *et al.* on behalf of the FACTOID group. (2021). Acceptance and Commitment Therapy for late-life treatment-resistant generalised anxiety: A feasibility study. *Age and Ageing*, 50(5), 1751–1761.

Gould, R. L., Rawlinson, C., Thompson, B. J., Weeks, K. and the COMMEND collaboration group. (2023). Acceptance and Commitment Therapy for people living with motor neuron disease: An uncontrolled feasibility study. *Pilot and Feasibility Studies*, 9, 116.

Gould, R. L., Thompson, B. J., Rawlinson, C., Kumar, P. *et al.* (2022). A randomised controlled trial of Acceptance and Commitment Therapy plus usual care compared to usual care alone for improving psychological health in people with motor neuron disease (COMMEND): Study protocol. *BMC Neurology*, 22, 431.

Harris, R. (2009). *ACT Made Simple: A Quick-Start Guide to ACT Basics and Beyond*. Oakland, CA: New Harbinger Publications.

Hayes, S. C., Strosahl, K. D. & Wilson, K. G. (2012). *Acceptance and Commitment Therapy: The Process and Practice of Mindful Change* (second edition). New York, NY: Guilford Press.

McCracken, L. M. (2021). Committed Action. In M. P. Twohig, M. E. Levin & J. M. Petersen (eds), *The Oxford Handbook of Acceptance and Commitment Therapy* (pp.295–310). Oxford: Oxford University Press.

Rolffs, J. L., Rogge, R. D. & Wilson, K. G. (2018). Disentangling components of flexibility via the hexaflex model: Development and validation of the multidimensional psychological flexibility inventory (MPFI). *Assessment*, 25(4), 458–482.

Scott, W., Chilcot, J., Guildford, B., Daly-Eichenhardt, A. & McCracken, L. M. (2018). Feasibility randomized controlled trial of online Acceptance and Commitment Therapy for patients with complex chronic pain in the United Kingdom. *European Journal of Pain*, 22(8), 1473–1484.

Stein, A. T., Carl, E., Cuijpers, P., Karyotaki, E. & Smits, J. A. J. (2020). Looking beyond depression: A meta-analysis of the effect of behavioral activation on depression, anxiety, and activation. *Psychological Medicine*, 51(9), 1491–1504.

Stoddard, J. A. & Afari, N. (2014). *The Big Book of ACT Metaphors: A Practitioner's Guide to Experiential Exercises and Metaphors in Acceptance and Commitment Therapy*. Oakland, CA: New Harbinger Publications.

Trompetter, H. R., ten Klooster, P. M., Schreurs, K. M. G., Fledderus, M., Westerhof, G. J. & Bohlmeijer, E. T. (2013). Measuring values and committed action with the Engaged Living Scale (ELS): Psychometric evaluation in a nonclinical sample and a chronic pain sample. *Psychological Assessment*, 25(4), 1235–1246.

Whiting, D. L., Simpson, G. K., Deane, F. P., Chuah, S. L., Maitz, M. & Weaver, J. (2021). Protocol for a phase two, parallel three-armed non-inferiority randomized controlled trial of Acceptance and Commitment Therapy (ACT-Adjust) comparing face-to-face and video conferencing delivery to individuals with traumatic brain injury experiencing psychological distress. *Frontiers in Psychology*, 12, 652323.

Appendices
Appendix 7.1: An example script of the Small Steps exercise

The aim of this exercise is to help you notice the potential barriers that automatically show up as soon as you think about what you could do to move towards the things that are important and matter to you. In this exercise I ask you to just consider the kind of actions or steps you could take to move towards being the type of person you want to be.

So, begin by bringing to mind one of your most important values...what you want to be doing...and how you want to be doing that...how you want to be acting or behaving.

And when you've got an idea about what this value is then just say it out aloud so that I know we can carry on with the rest of the exercise.

[If necessary, due to cognitive impairment, give a prompt with respect to the most important value.]

So now I invite you to consider an action or step that you could take to move you towards *[insert value]* within the next six months or so.

[If necessary, due to cognitive impairment, give a prompt with respect to this action or step.]

And now consider a smaller action or step that you could take to move you towards *[insert value]* within the next month or so.

[If necessary, due to cognitive impairment, give a prompt with respect to this action or step.]

And now consider an even smaller action or step that you could take to move you towards *[insert value]* within the next week or so.

[If necessary, due to cognitive impairment, give a prompt with respect to this action or step.]

Lastly, I invite you to consider the smallest action or step that you could take to move you towards *[insert value]* within the next day or so.

[If necessary, due to cognitive impairment, give a prompt with respect to this action or step.]

Become aware of whatever is showing up in your experience right now as you consider these actions or steps right now.

Notice what your mind is telling you...

Become aware of what feelings are around...

Notice what bodily sensations are here...and where they're showing up in the body.

See if you can notice any urges to try and control, change, avoid or get rid of these thoughts, feelings and bodily sensations...and if you can allow them to be just as they are right now.

And as we come to the last few moments of this exercise, I invite you to ask yourself, 'Am I willing to take my smallest step today or tomorrow to move me towards *[insert value]*?'

[If necessary, due to cognitive impairment, give a prompt with respect to this action or step.]

Note: If there are concerns that cognitive difficulties such as memory impairment might interfere with this exercise then elicit the small steps beforehand and then experientially complete this exercise.

Appendix 7.2: Goals, Actions and Values Plan incorporating selection, optimisation and compensation strategies

1. What do I want to do? What is my goal?

....
....
....
....

2. Why is this goal important to me? What type of person do I want to be alongside the difficulties I am experiencing? How do I want to be acting or behaving?

....
....
....
....

3. What difficulties with my health, financial, occupational, leisure or social situation get in the way of my goal?

....
....
....
....

4. How can I best focus my energy and resources on my goal? Select all that apply.

☐ Choose a goal that connects with a value that is the most important to me.
☐ Choose a goal that is in my best area of functioning.
☐ Adapt the goal so that it can be more realistically achieved.
☐ Replace the goal with another goal that can be more realistically achieved.

Further details:

....
....
....
....

5. How can I optimise or increase my chances of achieving my goal? Select all that apply.

☐ Learn a new skill.

☐ Practise a skill.

☐ Capitalise on what I can do or what I'm good at.

Further details:

. . . .

. . . .

. . . .

6. How can I compensate for difficulties with my health, financial, occupational, leisure or social situation in order that I can achieve my goal? Select all that apply.

☐ Seek support from elsewhere.

☐ Ask for help from others.

☐ Use equipment, aids or tools.

☐ Use physical or cognitive strategies to compensate for my difficulties.

Further details:

. . . .

. . . .

. . . .

7. What are the smallest actions or steps I can take to achieve my goal?

Goal:

Step 1:
- What?
- When by?

Step 2:
- What?
- When by?

Step 3:
- What?
- When by?

Step 4:
- What?
- When by?

Step 5:
- What?
- When by?

8. What potential barriers might get in the way of me achieving my goal? Potential barriers include:

- Financial, social, occupational or leisure barriers (e.g. not having enough time or money, lack of social support)
- Health-related barriers (e.g. difficulties with mobility, communication, memory problems, fatigue)
- Private or internal barriers (e.g. thoughts, feelings, images, memories, bodily sensations, urges)

How can I handle these potential barriers so that I can achieve my goal?

. . . .

. . . .

. . . .

. . . .

List each potential barrier	List ways of handling each potential barrier
. . . .	. . . .
. . . .	. . . .
. . . .	. . . .
. . . .	. . . .
. . . .	. . . .
. . . .	. . . .
. . . .	. . . .
. . . .	. . . .
. . . .	. . . .
. . . .	. . . .
. . . .	. . . .
. . . .	. . . .

Integrating Psychological Flexibility Processes in Acquired Neurological Conditions

Applications in a Context of Severe and Multiple Disadvantage

NIMA GOLIJANI-MOGHADDAM AND ANNA TICKLE

An introduction to us and our work

This chapter brings together the various processes that have been introduced over preceding chapters, to consider how 'psychological flexibility' can be harnessed when supporting people living with acquired neurological conditions (brain injuries and illnesses). For our illustrative case material, we present examples from within a context of severe and multiple disadvantage, highlighting the potential applicability of psychological flexibility processes in cases with people with complex needs requiring multi-agency working.

Nima: I work on a clinical psychology training programme in the UK, providing supervision and teaching on ACT (as a model that explicitly targets and integrates psychological flexibility processes), and conducting research developing, implementing and evaluating ACT and other process-based therapies – including for people living with acquired neurological conditions (stroke, multiple sclerosis, Alzheimer's disease; e.g. Oates *et al.*, 2020; Proctor *et al.*, 2018; Robinson, De Boos & Moghaddam, 2023). Clinically, I am currently working with people recovering from major traumatic injury (including traumatic brain injury) as part of an interdisciplinary vocational rehabilitation programme – and I draw on ACT/psychological flexibility processes within this work. I have been an ACT researcher and practitioner for over 15 years and learned that the psychological flexibility model is most useful for finding workability in situations where people become stuck or are confronted with challenges that overwhelm previous ways of coping.

Anna: I work as a consultant clinical psychologist for a third-sector provider of homelessness and substance use services across the East Midlands, UK, and on a clinical psychology training programme. Having trained as a systemic practitioner, I was a late convert to ACT because of my critical resistance to individualised approaches to problems that often have social causes. When I moved into working with those facing severe and multiple disadvantage, I needed an approach that would allow me to engage individuals without them feeling pathologised. Training in ACT has transformed my practice and it has become integral to my approach to life. It resonates with staff I train to use it and the people they work with.

The importance of psychological flexibility and using an integrated approach for people with neurological conditions

While previous chapters have mapped psychological flexibility in terms of constituent processes, it is important to consider these processes together – recognising (and mobilising) ways in which they may interact and influence each other. In practice, working with one process of psychological flexibility will typically intersect with other processes. This is consistent with their conceptual interdependence (Chin & Hayes, 2017) and empirical research finding strong associations among psychological flexibility processes, both in general and neurological populations (Pakenham *et al.*, 2024; Rolffs, Rogge & Wilson, 2018). Practically, we observe that the usefulness of one process often relies on or serves the others. For example, improving skills in cognitive defusion can make it easier to practise acceptance, which in turn can enhance the ability to stay present and connected with the here-and-now experience. Similarly, cultivating acceptance is best understood as a *means* of promoting valued actions – acceptance is not an end (Hayes, Pistorello & Levin, 2012), and this can be an important point to clarify when introducing acceptance-focused strategies (which can be misconstrued as advocating passivity). Self-as-context is a process that is sometimes conceptualised as a vehicle for other processes: a vantage point from which clients can take perspective on (versus through) their experiences (a 'helicopter view') that enables some distance from passing thoughts, feelings and sensations (*defusion* and *acceptance*) and potentiates more adaptive (vs. reactive) responses (*committed action on values*).

What do we mean by 'psychological flexibility'? How can we talk about this ability with clients?

We have broadly defined psychological flexibility as the ability to recognise and adapt to situational demands and affordances in pursuit of personally meaningful longer-term outcomes (Dawson & Golijani-Moghaddam, 2020).[1] With clients, we describe psychological flexibility as the capacity to make the best of situations, even those that are challenging – clarifying that this involves acknowledging and adjusting to challenging situations while still pursuing personally significant goals and objectives. Being psychologically flexible requires that we are present and aware enough to see what a situation brings ('What is happening here and now?') and have a guiding sense of what is important to us in the longer term ('How can I move towards

---

[1]   There are evident overlaps here with neuropsychological concepts of self-regulation and 'executive functioning' (Cherry *et al.*, 2021). As previous chapter authors have noted, acquired neurological conditions are often accompanied by difficulties with self-regulation, making psychological flexibility an apt target for development, but also an ability that may be subject to limitations or requiring of adaptations and additional scaffolding.

what matters in this situation?'). Importantly, being psychologically flexible also requires an openness to experiencing (and potentially harnessing) difficult thoughts and feelings – without trying to avoid or control them in ways that can stop us from being present and doing what matters.

Psychological studies over many years have consistently shown that avoiding unwanted thoughts, feelings and situations only worsens our mental health and wellbeing (Akbari *et al.*, 2022; Goodman *et al.*, 2019). The more we try to suppress these distressing experiences, the more they occupy our minds. This leads to inflexible behaviour and decision-making, where we are more focused on quick, temporary fixes rather than addressing the root of our discomfort. These short-term solutions may seem effective, but they prevent us from dealing with the underlying issues that can bring about meaningful, long-lasting change. We end up repeating these quick fixes because they give immediate relief, even though they don't contribute to long-term wellness.

In the context of an acquired neurological condition, such psychological *inflexibility* can significantly contribute to suffering. Perseverative efforts to deny, avoid, hide or control new limitations can lead to increased frustration and distress, and may be detrimental to recovery or adjustment – for example, through limiting engagement with rehabilitative therapies, communication with support systems and receptivity to adaptations (trying out new approaches to problem-solving and managing everyday tasks). Conversely, profound changes can be fostered through a deceptively simple shift in stance: towards acknowledging and embracing the condition, along with its restrictions and challenges, without excessive judgement or resistance. Accepting the condition's presence and impact, and the limits of personal control over this, may enable clients and their carers to focus on what can be done, rather than what can't be. This focus on possibility affords a more adaptive and accommodating approach to new realities – for example, finding novel ways to engage with valued activities or adjusting expectations for self in the circumstances of the condition. In concert, psychological flexibility processes can equip people with acquired neurological conditions to navigate challenges more effectively, through:

- figuring out what is most important to them (*values*) and how they can live in ways that reflect these priorities (*committed action*)

- working through potential barriers, such as unhelpful thoughts (*defusion*) and self-stories (*self-as-context*), unwanted feelings and physical sensations (*acceptance*), and inattention to opportunities for connecting with what matters (*present moment awareness*).

In common with more recent conceptualisation (Hayes *et al.*, 2011) and measurement modelling (Francis, Dawson & Golijani-Moghaddam, 2016), we conceive of psychological flexibility in terms of three core abilities (the 'triflex' of dyadic processes) which form malleable targets for intervention:

1. Openness to Experience: *acceptance and willingness* (Chapter 2) and *defusion* (Chapter 3) processes are targeted to foster a non-judgemental and detached relationship to internal experiences (**being open**).

2. Behavioural Awareness: *present moment awareness* (Chapter 4) and *self-as-context* (Chapter 5) processes are targeted to enhance a person's understanding of their actions and the experiential context in which they occur, leading to more mindful and deliberative behaviour (**being aware**).

3. Valued Action: *values* (Chapter 6) and *committed action* (Chapter 7) processes are targeted to promote actions that are aligned with personal values, encouraging behaviours that are fulfilling and life-enhancing (**being engaged**).[2]

---

2   With psychologist colleagues, we sometimes talk informally about cultivating psychological flexibility as a process of 'exposure and response selection': confronting internal experiences and external situations with openness and awareness (exposure) to enable deliberate, values-guided choices (response selection).

Formulating responses[3] in terms of these three core abilities can help to quickly identify areas for development (aspects of rigidity – being closed, unaware and disengaged) and strengths (aspects of flexibility) to be leveraged and reinforced. We provide a triflex formulation template in Appendix 8A and demonstrate use of this template with two case examples (later in this chapter). While our examples show this template applied to make sense of current client and broader systemic material, the formulation can be iteratively developed over time or made more specific in its focus – for example, formulating flexibility in pursuit of a particular valued goal or zooming in to the level of a single session (what in-session behaviours are coming up that could be usefully worked with?). The template can be adapted to create a shared formulation with clients, to support self-formulation (recognising the importance of our own ability to be open, aware and engaged with our clients (Wilson, 2009)), or to scaffold discussions in clinical supervision. Our process-focused approach to formulation enables broad applicability, supporting integration and translation between the theoretical elements of psychological flexibility and practice-based material.

A central metaphor or narrative can be helpful for connecting clients with the core components of psychological flexibility – linking abstract concepts to vivid, relatable imagery. There are many published examples, with shared essential themes, and the resonance and appropriateness of a particular metaphor will vary from person to person – as always, it's advisable to think about function (how effectively is this landing with the client?) and not get too attached to specific forms. One example we'll share is the metaphor of 'walking your own path' or 'hiking your own trail', which represents a journey of adaptation, resilience and personal growth, emphasising the importance of being open (embracing the 'new normal', however fluctuating), aware (staying mindful of current internal states and

---

3   Formulation can be broadly understood as the process and product of applying psychological concepts to understand the mainsprings of experienced difficulties and identify helpful ways of responding (Dawson & Moghaddam, 2015). Formulations are constructed, tested and adjusted through ongoing processes of deduction (drawing from, and applying, psychological theory) and induction (grounded in case-specific information).

external conditions) and engaged (actively living life in the context of personal abilities and values, despite challenges faced). A strength of the metaphor of 'hiking your own trail' is that (in common with ideas of *driving the bus* or *sailing your boat*) it offers an overarching *word picture* within which we can integrate specific processes (e.g. defusing from the 'rules' in guidebooks and advice from other hikers).

Navigating a trail with a neurological injury or illness might mean encountering unexpected and difficult terrain or abrupt weather changes. ***Being open*** in this context involves accepting and facing these unique challenges, rather than denying or avoiding them. It's about acknowledging the reality of the condition, associated emotions, and any condition-related limitations, much like acknowledging the rugged parts of a trail and preparing to navigate them. Hiking a trail also requires awareness of the immediate environment – the path underfoot, the weather, the wildlife. For someone with a neurological condition, ***being aware*** can particularly translate to a heightened appreciation of their current physical and emotional state. It implies being attuned to the body's signals, recognising limits and understanding emotional responses without being overly focused on how things were before the injury or illness, or how they might be in the future. Finally, just as a hiker engages with the journey, choosing paths that align with their destination and abilities, *being engaged* for someone with a neurological condition means actively participating in their own life. This involves setting realistic, value-driven goals and taking steps towards them. It is about adapting activities and goals to fit the 'new normal', finding new ways to engage in meaningful activities, and not letting the condition completely dictate the course of their life.

The notion of 'hiking your own trail' enables discussions around self-pacing and negotiating others' expectations (who is determining where the client is going, and how they should get there?) as well as consideration of values that underpin the journey. For example, values of connection, family and friendship may shape the meaning of 'hiking your own trail' to reflect a more interconnected view of autonomy – emphasising that, while paths are personally chosen, they are profoundly shaped, enriched and supported by relationships with others. The metaphor is useful for considering *workability* (i.e. the practical effectiveness of particular actions in relation to longer-term values-based goals): for example, some paths may seem more inviting or easier to traverse, but take the client 'off track'/away from where they want to be. Is the client willing to choose the path that takes them in their valued direction, even if it's a more challenging route? Similarly, the metaphor provides a good basis for discussions around accepting uncertainties or discomfort in service of moving forward (how long will we spend preparing for our hike or sheltering from inclement weather before we can recommence the journey? When does 'waiting for the right conditions' become costly avoidance?).

Building psychological flexibility can also be helpfully discussed in terms of 'learning to use the right tool for the job'. Just as using the right tool requires understanding the task at hand and choosing the most effective tool, psychological flexibility involves recognising what is needed in each context and responding appropriately. Similarly, just as using the same tool for every job is ineffective, applying the same response to every situation is not practical. Psychological flexibility is about moving away from rigid patterns of thinking and behaving, recognising that different situations call for different responses. One of the useful implications of this metaphor is that we need an extensive repertoire of behaviours to facilitate effective, situational responding – and that our tools (ways of responding) are not inherently 'good' or 'bad', but perhaps more/less workable for a given situation. Even behaviours that are often labelled 'avoidant' (distraction and disengagement) can be useful, particularly in the short-term and as part of a broader coping repertoire (Dawson & Golijani-Moghaddam, 2020). Again, the workability of each contextual response (tool for the job) can be explored in terms of both short- and long-term effectiveness (vs. costliness) for moving towards valued goals.

What is the evidence for targeting psychological flexibility?

The potential significance of psychological flexibility in the context of acquired neurological conditions is supported by well-defined theoretical arguments, as discussed previously and in preceding chapters. Additionally, empirical research indicates that, generally, higher levels of psychological flexibility correlate with better psychological health outcomes in individuals with neurological conditions (e.g. Faulkner *et al.*, 2023; Meek *et al.*, 2022). However, the evidence supporting a causal mediating role of psychological flexibility in these outcomes is still limited.

While evidence for the efficacy of ACT could be taken as empirical support for the value of promoting psychological flexibility, there is a critical distinction between evincing outcome effectiveness versus the putative change processes of ACT. Studies have shown positive effects of ACT on outcomes for people with acquired neurological conditions *in the absence of measurable changes in psychological flexibility* (Rauwenhoff *et al.*, 2023; Thompson *et al.*, 2022; Whiting *et al.*, 2020). Where ACT *has* been shown to influence ACT-targeted process variables in participants with neurological conditions, effects have generally been detected for narrow measures of pain acceptance rather than psychological flexibility more broadly (Han, Wilroy & Yuen, 2023). At face value, we might take this evidence (i.e. clearer effects of ACT interventions on outcome versus process variables) as challenging to the notion that psychological flexibility is a critical active ingredient for therapeutic change. Alternatively, such findings may reflect measurement issues (problems with the construct validity and change-responsivity of commonly used psychological flexibility measures); certainly, these measures are often generic/global, which may make them less apt to track flexible responding in condition- and individual-specific contexts – and psychological flexibility is really something that can only be understood contextually (as our ability to effectively adapt our behaviour to different situational demands, in service of personally meaningful longer-term goals). In research applications of ACT with neurological populations, we commonly use qualitative methods (e.g. post-treatment interviews by independent evaluators) to address questions regarding therapy change processes, and these methods have highlighted potential changes in psychological flexibility that were not apparent in self-report measures (Meek *et al.*, 2021; Robinson *et al.*, 2023).

Monitoring changes in psychological flexibility

In-depth interviewing is rarely a feasible approach for tracking psychological flexibility in practice, so what measures might we use for monitoring this ability and our efforts to promote it? Although the AAQ-II is the most used process measure in studies of ACT for people with acquired neurological conditions (Foote *et al.*, 2023), we caution against its use as a measure of 'psychological flexibility' given known issues with construct and discriminant validity (narrow capture of acceptance/experiential avoidance, versus psychological flexibility more broadly, and conflation with measurement of distress; Garner & Golijani-Moghaddam, 2021). We developed the CompACT as an alternative, more comprehensive measure of psychological flexibility (Francis *et al.*, 2016) and it has relative strengths in terms of discriminant validity (Ong *et al.*, 2020). In people with acquired neurological conditions, the CompACT has demonstrated acceptability (Giovannetti *et al.*, 2022) and treatment responsiveness (e.g. Ooi & Steverson, 2023). The recently validated ten-item version (Golijani-Moghaddam *et al.*, 2023) may be most suitable for clinical use, given its brevity; we include a version in Appendix 8B and encourage adaptations to make the questions accessible to clients with diverse cognitive abilities. Another measure that we have started to use is the Personalized Psychological Flexibility Index (Kashdan *et al.*, 2020). This measure explicitly examines flexibility of responding in relation to a personally meaningful life goal for the client, making it apt for values-based goal setting in rehabilitation contexts, and logically reflecting the conditional nature of psychological flexibility (e.g. openness and awareness as means to valued ends).

Practice applications: Psychological flexibility work in the context of acquired neurological conditions and severe and multiple disadvantage

It is important to set the scene of severe and multiple disadvantage (SMD), a term now used by the UK government to mean experiencing combinations of homelessness, substance use, offending (broader definitions also consider contact with the criminal justice system as victims), mental health difficulties and domestic and sexual violence and abuse. Empirical evidence connects each SMD criterion to brain injury, with particular focus on traumatic brain injury (TBI). TBI has been described as 'an underappreciated factor in the health trajectories of homeless and marginally housed individuals' (Stubbs *et al.*,

2020, p.e19) and a 'silent epidemic' among people in contact with the law (Kent & Williams, 2021, p.4). Substance use can be both a cause of brain injury and consequence that limits recovery (Taylor *et al.*, 2003). Substance use might also be a coping response to the mental health problems consequent to TBI (Howlett, Nelson & Stein, 2022), with growing evidence that individuals with TBI may be uniquely susceptible to opioid misuse (Adams, Corrigan & Dams-O'Connor, 2020). Accidental and deliberate overdoses and attempted suicide by hanging may also lead to TBI. Finally, while substance use is often researched in terms of the direct impact on the brain, interpersonal interactions related to buying illicit drugs frequently include violent assault. Both SMD and brain injury are also gendered. Generally, the effects of both biological sex and gender are underappreciated in TBI research and practice (Mollayeva, Mollayeva & Colantonio, 2018) but gendered responses may be needed to assess both risk of and recovery from brain injury. Domestic abuse often involves repeated injury to the head, neck and face, and 33 per cent of women offenders report TBI preceding their first offence, many from domestic violence (The Disabilities Trust, 2019). Both cis gender and transgender women who engage in sex work (many of whom face SMD) report a high prevalence of head injury related to violence in sex work, together with widespread stigma and discrimination as barriers to care (Baumann *et al.*, 2019).

While there is still much necessity for research and development of clinical practice in relation to SMD and TBI, the existing evidence of the relationship between complex individual and social circumstances and TBI presents a convincing case for attention to rehabilitation at the earliest possible point. Early intervention would not only benefit individuals but also wider society in mitigating the potential sequelae of TBI associated with SMD. While a focus on promoting psychological flexibility – via ACT – cannot mitigate social disadvantage, it can form an important component of support for both individuals and the systems around them. ACT's process-based, transdiagnostic approach allows some stepping back from complex histories and current circumstances, and a platform from which people can take steps towards a different future.

Adaptations for those with brain injury who are facing SMD

Previous chapters have outlined examples of adapting ACT practice for people with neurological conditions, and we concur with all the suggestions. Within this section, we focus on our more specific field of working with brain injury in the context of marginalised populations facing severe and multiple disadvantage. However, many of these adaptations will be relevant for working with other populations.

Embedding ACT to create a psychologically informed environment

Chapter 5 highlighted the role of the family system in supporting self-as-context work. For those facing SMD, who often do not have stable contact with family, it is vitally important to also consider wider multi-agency professional systems. Curvis and Methley (2022) highlight the potential for systemic thinking in the application of ACT for those with brain injury. Anna has started to develop systemic application of ACT within homelessness services, and this perhaps has particular significance in relation to those with brain injury or other neurological conditions that might impact direct engagement with staff.

Psychologically informed environments (PIEs) (Johnson, 2023) and trauma-informed care (TIC) are two complementary organisational approaches with potential for services supporting those with neurological conditions (e.g. Nemeth *et al.*, 2023). PIEs can be developed flexibly based on any psychological model. In Anna's organisation, ACT has evolved as the model of choice due to the positive reception of its principles and practice by service users and staff at all levels (sessions for senior leaders, other staff members, the staff wellbeing service, and direct work with service users). ACT allows a non-pathologising approach for survivors of trauma (McLean & Follette, 2016), which does not require detailed exploration of traumatic experiences. This is important for staff who do not feel equipped to work psychologically with trauma and for service users who may suddenly move on from services (e.g. due to eviction from temporary accommodation, hospitalisation or imprisonment).

The rationale for training staff teams and multi-agency systems to understand ACT is fourfold:

1. To influence how they work with individuals.
2. To consolidate the individual's work in therapy (and not contradict learning from ACT).
3. To manage their own responses to challenging work.
4. To build the organisational psychological flexibility of the system/s around the person.

Staff teams have been shown to change the way they work with people when trained to understand and formulate those they support (Buckley, Tickle & McDonald, 2021). Without understanding the principles of ACT, staff could easily misconstrue a therapist's direction to 'sit with difficult thoughts or feelings' as unhelpful, unnecessary or even cruel. It is common for staff to offer reassurance or thought challenging if somebody reports distressing thoughts, or to support the use of distraction techniques, counter to cultivating skills underpinning psychological flexibility. There is also widespread awareness of 'emotional regulation' skills, which staff might use with individuals in distress. Although emotional regulation might be part of ACT, within most intervention models it serves purposes that contradict ACT principles (Harris, 2020). Thus, staff teaching 'emotion regulation' strategies may try to encourage control of emotional experience in ways that antithetically promote inflexibility. Beyond preventing inadvertent undermining of ACT principles, embedding understanding across the organisation allows staff to actively support promotion of psychological flexibility: for example, helping the individual to be open, aware and engaged in everyday situations.

Organisational documentation commonly involves history taking, risk assessment and future planning to an extent that encourages people to be both past- and future-focused (rather than present moment aware) and regularly connected to 'self-as-content' – the psychologically inflexible stories about self that limit possibilities for change (e.g. 'I am... risky/disabled/incapable/a burden/an addict'). Psychological inflexibility can be perpetuated by deficit-focused approaches; for example, although services relentlessly try to get people to take action (take part in meaningful activity, stop drug use, secure a tenancy, make use of mental health support, etc.), this is rarely connected to the individual's values, despite the wish of people facing SMD to receive values-focused support (Buckley *et al.*, in press). Unvalued and unrealistic goals can add layers of unwanted thoughts, feelings and experiences (disappointment, failure, shame, etc.) to become fused with, making future attempts at committed action aversive.

Working with marginalised and traumatised individuals within under-resourced professional and social systems can take a toll on anybody. This might manifest in ways variously labelled as 'work-related stress', 'vicarious trauma', 'moral injury' or 'burnout'. Training staff to use ACT skills themselves can reduce the likelihood of compassion fatigue and burnout (Reeve *et al.*, 2021). This can be done from the perspective of 'staff wellbeing' but can also be interwoven through conversations about service users, to help staff step back from work often described as 'firefighting' the crises presented by those they support. It is vital to recognise that sometimes it is collections of multi-agency professionals around a person (the system) that can be psychologically inflexible. This can manifest as a collective fusion with beliefs about either a person (e.g. 'They are too complex for our service'; 'They are not ready for change') or the system (e.g. 'Everything possible has been tried'; 'We are stuck'; 'We can't work in the way needed'), together with an unwillingness to sit with organisational emotion such as anxiety related to positive risk taking or trying new things. Organisations understandably want to experientially avoid risk but this can be fused with ideas that they can 'control' and 'prevent' risk, sometimes leading to the use of approaches that exert power over people and contradict principles of psychologically and trauma-informed work.

The multi-agency system might need to be collectively guided through 'creative hopelessness' and exercises that integrate the six ACT processes in work to develop collective psychological flexibility to enable new and creative approaches to work, particularly when the system or individual appears 'stuck'. Weatherhead, Curvis and

Rosebert (2021) offer further detailed discussion of how ACT might be used systemically in homelessness services to think about individuals with brain injury.

Sensitivity to context and resource

Understanding the pre-injury context, including intersectional and stigmatised identities, is vital. People facing SMD have often internalised deficit-focused stories about them, rather than having lost an idealised sense of self because of TBI. Consequently, self-as-context work is likely to focus less directly on brain injury and more on a conceptualised self related to stigmatised identities (e.g. 'I am an addict').

Trauma (historical and ongoing) and substance use can both impact somebody's ability to be present moment focused and tolerate overwhelming feelings of hyper- or hypo-arousal. Work to develop skills in openness and awareness needs to carefully account for this and what is workable for an individual. For instance, while substance use often serves a function of experiential avoidance, and many therapists prefer their clients to be sober during sessions, there are cases where a person might only be able to manage their emotions effectively enough to attend appointments if they are somewhat under the influence initially. A judgement may need to be made about whether (and for whom) that is more workable than not allowing access to therapy.

It is important for therapists to be sensitive to resources and context. As authors of other chapters have said, metaphors should be chosen carefully. 'Hiking your own trail' offers relative neutrality (e.g. compared to analogies around driving, which is out of reach financially for many facing SMD), but might require further consideration or adaptation for those with mobility issues. Similarly, pictures used on values cards, or assumptions about resources in present moment awareness exercises, need deliberation. Present moment awareness exercises based on regular activities are likely to be much more effective for this group than guided scripts or longer practices, particularly when people do not have access to devices for playing recorded guidance.

CASE STUDIES ILLUSTRATING INTEGRATED PRACTICE

The case studies used here are fictional to prevent identification of individuals, but closely represent typical realities of people Anna has worked with and ACT implementation by Anna and colleagues.

Case study: Joanna

Joanna is a 29-year-old residing in a hostel for women facing SMD. Little is known about her early history, other than that she has used heroin since being a teenager. She has very occasional contact with her mother and sister. Her sister currently has parental responsibility for Joanna's ten-year-old daughter, who was taken from Joanna's care five years ago. Joanna began living in the area when released homeless from prison.

Last year, Joanna had a stroke. As is often the case for those facing SMD, the current system around her was not involved at the time and has not been able to acquire information from the hospital trust about assessments or treatment. Joanna has muscle weakness affecting her hand, arm and face, and requires adapted cutlery and a beaker to prevent drooling. It is unknown whether she has other ongoing effects of the stroke, as Joanna is very avoidant of staff in the hostel. She does not keep to appointments for support planning sessions, continues to inject heroin daily, eats very little, and sex works for income. She reports being regularly punched in the face by 'punters'. Joanna has said that she wants to go back to prison to 'give my body a break'. Joanna is very low in mood and self-neglectful. While services might observe her to organise her life around her heroin use, from an ACT (i.e. psychological flexibility-informed) perspective this would be viewed as being organised around experiential avoidance. Joanna does not, or cannot, articulate any aspirations for even the short-term future. A formulation is presented in Appendix 8C.

Case study: Liam

Liam is a 48-year-old residing in a hostel for men facing SMD. He is very well known to services, having been in and out of hostels, interspersed with periods in prison, sleeping rough and 'sofa surfing'.

Liam had a close relationship with his parents, although both were alcohol dependent and are deceased, as are his brothers. Pre-injury, Liam has done casual work and had long-term partners, with whom he shared tenancies and fathered children. When his relationship broke down and he became homeless, Liam was admitted to psychiatric hospital for two weeks and given a diagnosis of emotionally unstable personality disorder. Since then, he has been supported to secure multiple tenancies but lost them all through imprisonment or eviction due to antisocial behaviour, including threatening behaviour towards neighbours.

As is often the case in homelessness services, the term 'brain injury' cannot be found in Liam's records, but a review of his notes evidences an extensive history of likely acquired or traumatic brain injury over the course of a decade. Incidents include multiple drug overdoses (accidental and deliberate), involving being revived by Naloxone and/or cardiopulmonary resuscitation; a suicide attempt by hanging, thwarted by somebody cutting the ligature; and serious assaults, some by multiple men involving blunt objects to Liam's head and in one case his head being stamped on. Although these are extreme, similar histories are not uncommon for those facing SMD.

Liam struggles to attend formal appointments (including those required by Probation to avoid recall to prison) but loves to chat informally with staff on shift in the hostel. Liam sees himself as a failure and at times expresses a wish to die, but can equally enjoy laughing, joking, singing and dancing, and talks about wanting his own place, to stop using drugs, and to have contact with his now adult children. Liam will report very positive outcomes of appointments with professionals to hostel staff, which are not in line with the professional's account of the appointment. This is often viewed as Liam exaggerating the truth to appear favourable, but it could represent confabulation. A formulation is presented in Appendix 8D. Appendix 8E offers an example of how the framework might further be used to formulate psychological flexibility in the broader system around Liam.

Approaches to working with Joanna and Liam to build psychological flexibility

We offer the two contrasting cases to show that the elements of psychological flexibility can always be integrated, but that the focus on each element may vary according to case-specific needs. The emphasis on individual versus indirect work might also differ. In Joanna's case, engagement would need to be slowly developed and supported through staff in the hostel taking regular opportunities for brief interactions informed by ACT principles. Although Joanna clearly needs support to identify values, her level of avoidance is such that she would likely need support to develop skills relating to being open and aware, prior to being able to engage with discussion about values. A common ACT saying is that 'in our pain we find our values, in our values we find our pain'. For Joanna, we might predict that being put in touch with what is important to her might lead to overwhelming feelings of loss, grief and shame. Building skills in acceptance, defusion and present moment awareness may be necessary to support integrated work involving the broader triflex.

For Liam, who can clearly express his values, work might start with a focus on values: motivating him to develop the openness and awareness skills that would support him to act on his values (by enabling more effective responses to interfering experiences of low mood or judgemental thoughts). Staff would likely be less involved in this work, other than offering practical support around attending appointments. In supporting individuals like Liam, hostel staff use whiteboards with weekly plans within people's bedrooms, ensure they remind people of appointments on morning welfare checks, and support problem-solving about how to get to appointments. Agencies communicating the results of appointments with each other would also be beneficial, as it would assist Liam in remembering these outcomes. Professionals in appointments might also write down key bullet points for Liam at the end of an appointment. It might be possible to use a client-centred version of the triflex formulation with Liam. Similarly, the ACT Matrix (Polk *et al.*, 2016) can offer an alternative tool for drawing together the six processes in direct work. Anna has sometimes used this as an assessment tool in early sessions, but for other clients it has been a useful tool later in therapy, to draw together discussions across sessions. Appendix 8F offers an example of how a matrix might be developed with Liam.

References

Adams, R. S., Corrigan, J. D. & Dams-O'Connor, K. (2020). Opioid use among individuals with traumatic brain injury: A perfect storm? *Journal of Neurotrauma*, 37(1), 211–216.

Akbari, M., Seydavi, M., Hosseini, Z. S., Krafft, J. & Levin, M. E. (2022). Experiential avoidance in depression, anxiety, obsessive-compulsive related, and posttraumatic stress disorders: A comprehensive systematic review and meta-analysis. *Journal of Contextual Behavioral Science*, 24, 65–78. https://doi.org/https://doi.org/10.1016/j.jcbs.2022.03.007

Baumann, R. M., Hamilton-Wright, S., Riley, D. L., Brown, K. *et al.* (2019). Experiences of violence and head injury among women and transgender women sex workers. *Sexuality Research and Social Policy*, 16(3), 278–288. https://doi.org/10.1007/s13178-018-0334-0

Buckley, S., Tickle, A., Dawson, D. & Eagle, R. (in press). 'My values keep me well… would they help other people?': A thematic analysis exploring the values and valued behaviours of people facing severe and multiple disadvantage. *International Journal on Homelessness*.

Buckley, S., Tickle, A. & McDonald, S. (2021). Implementing psychological formulation into complex needs homeless hostels to develop a psychologically informed environment. *Journal of Social Distress and Homelessness*, 30(2), 164–173. https://doi.org/10.1080/10530789.2020.1786922

Cherry, K. M., Hoeven, E. V., Patterson, T. S. & Lumley, M. N. (2021). Defining and measuring 'psychological flexibility': A narrative scoping review of diverse flexibility and rigidity constructs and perspectives. *Clinical Psychology Review*, 84, 101973. https://doi.org/https://doi.org/10.1016/j.cpr.2021.101973

Chin, F. & Hayes, S. C. (2017). Chapter 7: Acceptance and Commitment Therapy and the Cognitive Behavioral Tradition: Assumptions, Model, Methods, and Outcomes. In S. G. Hofmann & G. J. G. Asmundson (eds), *The Science of Cognitive Behavioral Therapy* (pp.155–173). San Diego, CA: Academic Press.

Curvis, W. & Methley, A. (2022). *Acceptance and Commitment Therapy and Brain Injury. A Practical Guide for Clinicians*. London: Routledge.

Dawson, D. & Moghaddam, N. G. (2015). *Formulation in Action*. Warsaw, Poland: De Gruyter.

Dawson, D. L. & Golijani-Moghaddam, N. (2020). COVID-19: Psychological flexibility, coping, mental health, and wellbeing in the UK during the pandemic. *Journal of Contextual Behavioral Science*, 17, 126–134. https://doi.org/https://doi.org/10.1016/j.jcbs.2020.07.010

Faulkner, J. W., Snell, D. L., Theadom, A., Mahon, S. & Barker-Collo, S. (2023). The influence of psychological flexibility on persistent post concussion symptoms and functional status after mild traumatic brain injury. *Disability and Rehabilitation*, 45(7), 1192–1201. https://doi.org/10.1080/09638288.2022.2055167

Foote, H., Bowen, A., Cotterill, S., Hill, G., Pieri, M. & Patchwood, E. (2023). A scoping review to identify process and outcome measures used in acceptance and commitment therapy research, with adults with acquired neurological conditions. *Clinical Rehabilitation*, 37(6), 808–835. https://doi.org/10.1177/02692155221144554

Francis, A. W., Dawson, D. L. & Golijani-Moghaddam, N. (2016). The development and validation of the Comprehensive Assessment of Acceptance and Commitment Therapy processes (CompACT). *Journal of Contextual Behavioral Science*, 5(3), 134–145.

Garner, E. V. & Golijani-Moghaddam, N. (2021). Relationship between psychological flexibility and work-related quality of life for healthcare professionals: A systematic review and meta-analysis. *Journal of Contextual Behavioral Science*, 21, 98–112. https://doi.org/https://doi.org/10.1016/j.jcbs.2021.06.007

Giovannetti, A. M., Pöttgen, J., Anglada, E., Menéndez, R. *et al.* (2022). Cross-country adaptation of a psychological flexibility measure: The comprehensive assessment of Acceptance and Commitment Therapy processes. *International Journal of Environmental Research and Public Health*, 19(6), 3150. www.mdpi.com/1660-4601/19/6/3150

Golijani-Moghaddam, N., Morris, J. L., Bayliss, K. & Dawson, D. L. (2023). The CompACT-10: Development and validation of a Comprehensive assessment of Acceptance and Commitment Therapy processes short-form in representative UK samples. *Journal of Contextual Behavioral Science*, 29, 59–66. https://doi.org/https://doi.org/10.1016/j.jcbs.2023.06.003

Goodman, F. R., Kashdan, T. B., Larrazabal, M. A. & West, J. T. (2019). Experiential Avoidance. In B. O. Olatunji (ed.), *The Cambridge Handbook of Anxiety and Related Disorders* (pp.255–281). Cambridge, UK: Cambridge University Press. https://doi.org/DOI: 10.1017/9781108140416.010

Han, A., Wilroy, J. D. & Yuen, H. K. (2023). Effects of acceptance and commitment therapy on depressive symptoms, anxiety, pain intensity, quality of life, acceptance, and functional impairment in individuals with neurological disorders: A systematic review and meta-analysis. *Clinical Psychologist*, 27(2), 210–231. https://doi.org/10.1080/13284207.2022.2163158

Harris, R. (2020). *Emotion Regulation Strategies in ACT. A Practical Guide for ACT Therapists*. https://contextualconsulting.co.uk/wp-content/uploads/2020/02/Emotional-Regulation-in-ACT-Russ-Harris.pdf

Hayes, S. C., Pistorello, J. & Levin, M. E. (2012). Acceptance and commitment therapy as a unified model of behavior change. *The Counseling Psychologist*, 40(7), 976–1002.

Hayes, S. C., Villatte, M., Levin, M. & Hildebrandt, M. (2011). Open, aware, and active: Contextual approaches as an emerging trend in the behavioral and cognitive therapies. *Annual Review of Clinical Psychology*, 7, 141–168.

Howlett, J. R., Nelson, L. D. & Stein, M. B. (2022). Mental health consequences of traumatic brain injury. *Biological Psychiatry*, 91(5), 413–420.

Johnson, R. (2023). *Psychologically Informed Environments From the Ground Up. Service Design for Complex Needs*. Fertile Imagination.

Kashdan, T. B., Disabato, D. J., Goodman, F. R., Doorley, J. D. & McKnight, P. E. (2020). Understanding psychological flexibility: A multimethod exploration of pursuing valued goals despite the presence of distress. *Psychological Assessment*, 32(9), 829.

Kent, H. & Williams, H. (2021). *Traumatic Brain Injury*. Her Majesty's Inspectorate of Probation. https://hmiprobation.justiceinspectorates.gov.uk/document/traumatic-brain-injury

McLean, C. & Follette, V. M. (2016). Acceptance and commitment therapy as a non-pathologizing intervention approach for survivors of trauma. *Journal of Trauma & Dissociation*, 17(2), 138–150. https://doi.org/10.1080/15299732.2016.1103111

Meek, C., das Nair, R., Evangelou, N., Middleton, R., Tuite-Dalton, K. & Moghaddam, N. (2022). Psychological flexibility, distress, and quality of life in secondary progressive multiple sclerosis: A cross-sectional study. *Multiple Sclerosis and Related Disorders*, 67, 104154. https://doi.org/https://doi.org/10.1016/j.msard.2022.104154

Meek, C., Moghaddam, N. G., Evangelou, N., Oates, L. L. *et al.* (2021). Acceptance-based telephone support around the time of transition to secondary progressive multiple sclerosis: A feasibility randomised controlled trial. *Journal of Contextual Behavioral Science*, 21, 158–170. https://doi.org/https://doi.org/10.1016/j.jcbs.2021.07.001

Mollayeva, T., Mollayeva, S. & Colantonio, A. (2018). Traumatic brain injury: Sex, gender and intersecting vulnerabilities. *Nature Reviews Neurology*, 14(12), 711–722. https://doi.org/10.1038/s41582-018-0091-y

Nemeth, J., Ramirez, R., Debowski, C., Kulow, E. *et al.* (2023). The CARE Health Advocacy Intervention improves trauma-informed practices at domestic violence service organizations to address brain injury, mental health, and substance use. *The Journal of Head Trauma Rehabilitation*, 38(6), 439–447. https://doi.org/10.1097/htr.0000000000000871

Oates, L. L., Moghaddam, N., Evangelou, N. & das Nair, R. (2020). Behavioural activation treatment for depression in individuals with neurological conditions: A systematic review. *Clinical Rehabilitation*, 34(3), 310–319. https://doi.org/10.1177/0269215519896404

Ong, C. W., Pierce, B. G., Petersen, J. M., Barney, J. L. *et al.* (2020). A psychometric comparison of psychological inflexibility measures: Discriminant validity and item performance. *Journal of Contextual Behavioral Science*, 18, 34–47. https://doi.org/https://doi.org/10.1016/j.jcbs.2020.08.007

Ooi, J. & Steverson, T. (2023). Acceptance and commitment therapy (ACT) for post-stroke adjustment difficulties via telerehabilitation in a working-age man. *The Cognitive Behaviour Therapist*, 16, e31, Article e31. https://doi.org/10.1017/S1754470X23000260

Pakenham, K. I., Landi, G., Grandi, S. & Tossani, E. (2024). The mediating role of psychological flexibility in the relationship between resilience and distress and quality of life in people with multiple sclerosis. *Journal of Health Psychology*, 29(1), 65–80. https://doi.org/10.1177/13591053231182364

Polk, K. L., Schoendorff, B., Webster, M. & Olaz, F. O. (2016). *The Essential Guide to the ACT Matrix: A Step-By-Step Approach to Using the ACT Matrix Model in Clinical Practice*. Oakland, CA: New Harbinger Publications.

Proctor, B. J., Moghaddam, N., Vogt, W. & das Nair, R. (2018). Telephone psychotherapy in multiple sclerosis: A systematic review and meta-analysis. *Rehabilitation Psychology*, 63(1), 16–28. https://doi.org/10.1037/rep0000182

Rauwenhoff, J. C. C., Bol, Y., Peeters, F., van den Hout, A. J. H. C., Geusgens, C. A. V. & van Heugten, C. M. (2023). Acceptance and commitment therapy for individuals with depressive and anxiety symptoms following acquired brain injury: A non-concurrent multiple baseline design across four cases. *Neuropsychological Rehabilitation*, 33(6), 1018–1048. https://doi.org/10.1080/09602011.2022.2053169

Reeve, A., Moghaddam, N., Tickle, A. & Young, D. (2021). A brief acceptance and commitment intervention for work-related stress and burnout amongst frontline homelessness staff: A single case experimental design series. *Clinical Psychology & Psychotherapy*, 28(5), 1001–1019. https://doi.org/https://doi.org/10.1002/cpp.2555

Robinson, A., De Boos, D. & Moghaddam, N. (2023). Acceptance and commitment therapy (ACT) for people with dementia experiencing psychological distress: A hermeneutic single-case efficacy design (HSCED) series. *Counselling and Psychotherapy Research*, 23(4), 1108–1122. https://doi.org/https://doi.org/10.1002/capr.12646

Rolffs, J. L., Rogge, R. D. & Wilson, K. G. (2018). Disentangling components of flexibility via the Hexaflex Model: Development and validation of the Multidimensional Psychological Flexibility Inventory (MPFI). *Assessment*, 25(4), 458–482. https://doi.org/10.1177/1073191116645905

Stubbs, J. L., Thornton, A. E., Sevick, J. M., Silverberg, N. D. *et al.* (2020). Traumatic brain injury in homeless and marginally housed individuals: A systematic review and meta-analysis. *The Lancet Public Health*, 5(1), e19–e32.

Taylor, L. A., Kreutzer, J. S., Demm, S. R. & Meade, M. A. (2003). Traumatic brain injury and substance abuse: A review and analysis of the literature. *Neuropsychological Rehabilitation*, 13(1–2), 165–188. https://doi.org/10.1080/09602010244000336

The Disabilities Trust. (2019). *Making the link. Female offending and brain injury*. The Disabilities Trust. https://barrowcadbury.org.uk/our-impact/publications-and-research/making-the-link-female-offenders-and-brain-injury

Thompson, B., Moghaddam, N., Evangelou, N., Baufeldt, A. & das Nair, R. (2022). Effectiveness of acceptance and commitment therapy for improving quality of life and mood in individuals with multiple sclerosis: A systematic review and meta-analysis. *Multiple Sclerosis and Related Disorders*, 63, 103862.

Weatherhead, S., Curvis, W. & Rosebert, C. (2021). Using Acceptance and Commitment Therapy Principles to Support Systemic Change. In W. Curvis & A. Methley (eds), *Acceptance and Commitment Therapy and Brain Injury. A Practical Guide for Clinicians* (pp.165–181). London: Routledge.

Whiting, D., Deane, F., McLeod, H., Ciarrochi, J. & Simpson, G. (2020). Can acceptance and commitment therapy facilitate psychological adjustment after a severe traumatic brain injury? A pilot randomized controlled trial. *Neuropsychological Rehabilitation*, 30(7), 1348–1371. https://doi.org/10.1080/09602011.2019.1583582

Wilson, K. G. (2009). *Mindfulness for Two: An Acceptance and Commitment Therapy Approach to Mindfulness in Psychotherapy*. Oakland, CA: New Harbinger Publications.

Appendix 8A: Triflex formulation template

What do they want to move towards? (Identify values-based goals):

What experiences might get in the way? (Identify difficult situations, thoughts, feelings):

Open	Aware	Engaged

Closed	Unaware	Disengaged

Responses to teach, model, elicit, practise and reinforce

More workable ◄────────────► Less workable

APPENDIX 8B: CompACT-10 measure of psychological flexibility (Golijani-Moghaddam et al., 2023)

CompACT⁸

Name: .... Date: ....

Please rate the following 10 statements using the scale below:

0 Strongly disagree **1** Moderately disagree **2** Slightly disagree **3** Neither agree nor disagree **4** Slightly agree **5** Moderately agree **6** Strongly agree

	0	1	2	3	4	5	6
1. I rush through meaningful activities without being really attentive to them	0	1	2	3	4	5	6
2. I act in ways that are consistent with how I wish to live my life	0	1	2	3	4	5	6
3. I tell myself that I shouldn't have certain thoughts	0	1	2	3	4	5	6
4. I behave in line with my personal values	0	1	2	3	4	5	6
5. I go out of my way to avoid situations that might bring difficult thoughts, feelings or sensations	0	1	2	3	4	5	6
6. Even when doing the things that matter to me, I find myself doing them without paying attention	0	1	2	3	4	5	6
7. I undertake things that are meaningful to me, even when I find it hard to do so	0	1	2	3	4	5	6
8. I work hard to keep out upsetting feeling	0	1	2	3	4	5	6
9. It seems I am 'running on automatic' without much awareness of what I'm doing	0	1	2	3	4	5	6
10. I can keep going with something when it's important to me	0	1	2	3	4	5	6

Scoring instructions (administrative use only) REMOVE FOR CLIENTS

Scores are derived by summing responses for each of the three subscales (Openness to Experience; Behavioural Awareness; Valued Action) or the scale as a whole (CompACT Total score).

Six items are reverse-scored before summation (items 1, 3, 5, 6, 8 and 9).

Openness to Experience (OE) subscale

Calculated as the sum of scores for items: 3 (reversed), 5 (reversed) and 8 (reversed).

Subscale scores range from 0–18, with higher scores indicating greater openness to experience (willingness to experience internal events [thoughts, feelings, sensations, etc.] without trying to control or avoid them).

Behavioural Awareness (BA) subscale

Calculated as the sum of scores for items: 1 (reversed), 6 (reversed) and 9 (reversed).

Subscale scores range from 0–18 with higher scores indicating greater behavioural awareness (mindful attention to current actions).

Valued Action (VA) subscale

Calculated as the sum of scores for items: 2, 4, 7 and 10.

Subscale scores range from 0–24 with higher scores indicating greater engagement in valued actions (meaningful activity).

CompACT total

Calculated as the sum of the three subscale scores, the full-scale CompACT total score ranges from 0–60, with higher scores indicating greater psychological flexibility: The ability to attend and adapt to situational demands in the pursuit of personally-meaningful longer-term goals.

Appendix 8C: Tri-flex formulation for Joanna

What do they want to move towards? (Identify values-based goals):

Very hard to establish. Joanna is focused on what she wants to move away from (e.g. away from sex work, away from using drugs). However, Joanna's wish to go back to prison to give her body a break is reflected back to her as indicating a wish to move towards better health, and with further exploration her wishes to move away from sex work and drugs are framed as moves towards values of safety and self-respect.

What experiences might get in the way? (Identify difficult situations, thoughts, feelings): Thoughts: 'I deserve the stroke as punishment for addiction and failing my daughter'; 'I'm vulnerable to other women in the hostel as I can't physically stand up for myself'; 'Drooling makes me look like I'm stupid'.

Intense feelings of shame and hopelessness; flashbacks to multiple traumas and experiences of powerlessness, including during the stroke, treatment in hospital, and during sex work urges to use drugs to block out the thoughts, feelings and flashbacks.

	Open	Aware	Engaged
Responses to teach, model, elicit, practise and reinforce	• Despite working hard to block out painful thoughts, memories and feelings of shame, Joanna does manage to sit with high levels of anxiety and overcome thoughts about risk in daily situations involving real threat. This can be used as a starting point for thinking about skills of openness.	• Most present aware just before injecting. Can tune into the physical sensations before, during and immediately after, as well as the sights, smells and sounds of the ritual of preparing to inject.	• Has recently – and unusually – attended hospital due to concerns about an infection. • Has some engagement with harm reduction support (e.g. needle exchange).
Closed	• Ruminating at length about deserving the stroke. • Avoiding staff and any conversations about needs. • Daily use of drugs to block out thoughts and feelings.	• Past focused: Replaying traumatic memories, sometimes purposefully but at other times as flashbacks. • Future focused on next opportunity to score, and raising cash. • Stories of self as 'addict', 'vulnerable', 'disabled'. **Unaware**	• Cannot really imagine life without daily drug use, which predates becoming an adult. • Struggles to envisage how to enact 'safety', 'health' or 'self-respect' beyond basic harm reduction. **Disengaged**

More workable

Less workable

Appendix 8D: Tri-flex formulation for Liam (client-level)

What do they want to move towards? (Identify values-based goals):

A stable home; being clean and sober; building relationships with children; good friendships with people who don't use or drink.

What might get in the way? (Identify difficult situations, thoughts, feelings):

Struggling to remember appointments (sometimes genuinely forgetting, at other times predicting appointments will force focus on problems, which can lead to low mood, so allowing self to become 'distracted' by socialising and not making the appointment). Stories about self that give rise to unwanted feelings.

How flexibly are [you/they] responding to difficult experiences as they pursue their goals?

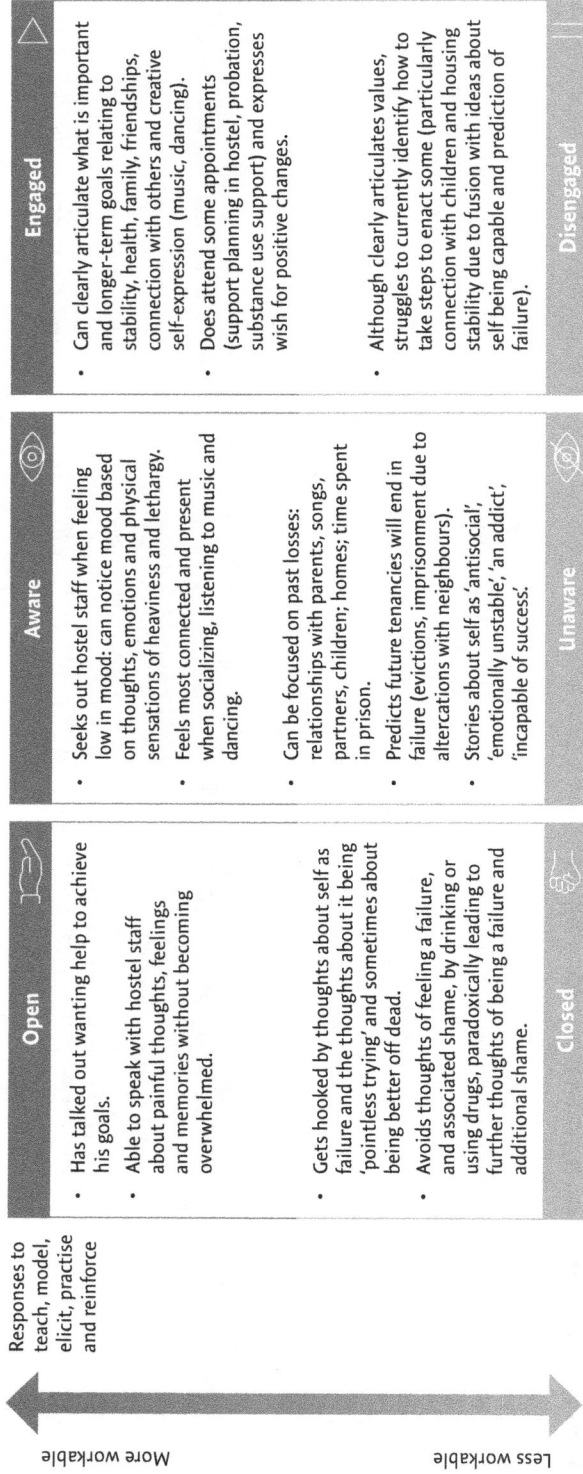

	Open 🖐	Aware 👁	Engaged △
Responses to teach, model, elicit, practise and reinforce	• Has talked out wanting help to achieve his goals. • Able to speak with hostel staff about painful thoughts, feelings and memories without becoming overwhelmed.	• Seeks out hostel staff when feeling low in mood: can notice mood based on thoughts, emotions and physical sensations of heaviness and lethargy. • Feels most connected and present when socializing, listening to music and dancing.	• Can clearly articulate what is important and longer-term goals relating to stability, health, family, friendships, connection with others and creative self-expression (music, dancing). • Does attend some appointments (support planning in hostel, probation, substance use support) and expresses wish for positive changes.
	Closed ✊	**Unaware** 👁̶	**Disengaged** ‖
	• Gets hooked by thoughts about self as failure and the thoughts about it being 'pointless trying' and sometimes about being better off dead. • Avoids thoughts of feeling a failure, and associated shame, by drinking or using drugs, paradoxically leading to further thoughts of being a failure and additional shame.	• Can be focused on past losses: relationships with parents, songs, partners, children; homes; time spent in prison. • Predicts future tenancies will end in failure (evictions, imprisonment due to altercations with neighbours). • Stories about self as 'antisocial', 'emotionally unstable', an addict', 'incapable of success.'	• Although clearly articulates values, struggles to currently identify how to take steps to enact some (particularly connection with children and housing stability due to fusion with ideas about self being capable and prediction of failure).

More workable ← → Less workable

Appendix 8E: Triflex formulation for Liam (staff-level)

What do they want to move towards? (Identify values-based goals):

Multi-agency system agencies and individuals want to offer person-centred support; address systemic inequalities and stigma: see Liam move towards increased quality of life in the form of housing stability, sobriety and healthy relationships.

What experiences might get in the way? (Identify difficult situations, thoughts, feelings):

Frustration with Liam when he misses appointments; frustration with serial systems (lack of flexibility re: appointments; lack of housing options but commissioner expectations of people moving through hostels quickly; easy availability of drugs and alcohol; stigma re drug use and personality disorder, lack of funding for or availability of consistent support for people with chronic but 'wild' or 'hidden' needs) and the negative impact of social systems on Liam's health and wellbeing.

How flexibly is the system responding to difficult experiences as they pursue their goals/support Liam to pursue his goals?

	Open	Aware	Engaged
Responses to teach, model, elicit, practise and reinforce	• Professionals recognise commissioning targets are unrealistic and sit with anxiety about not meeting them. We discuss multi-agency meetings, and realities of flexing rules for Liam, in case of future offending, suicide or harm from drug use. However, there is collective agreement to sit with short-term risk to promote long-term progress. • Individual agencies at times become very anxious about 'targets' and pressures of the system. • Individual staff members can get hooked by thoughts about risk and (partial) potential to end up 'in Coroner's court' if Liam dies. When expressed aloud, this anxiety can be contagious and lead to the system being much less tolerant of risk.	• Based on awareness of ACT and trauma-informed approaches in the system, staff do notice their internal pulls towards pressuring Liam. Staff can collectively notice and discuss this. • Meetings (multi-agency and individual appointments with Liam) can become dominated by his history, risk, past offending or diagnosis of personality disorder, particularly if Liam is talking about any of these. • All agencies at different times tend to predict failure for Liam, particularly in relation to managing tenancies or remaining abstinent.	• Very clear about their values and wish to work flexibly, bending the rules wherever possible to allow person-centred support (e.g. Probation willing to count phone contact despite requirement for face-to-face appointments to avoid recall, hostel staff calling multi-agency meetings to ensure Liam is at the centre of coordinated work and his views are considered). • When hooked by concerns about targets or risk, agencies can be pulled towards pressuring Liam into 'success' by 'convincing' or coercing him into sobriety (e.g. to 'do things by the book') and recall him to prison to reduce access to drugs. • There is acknowledgement in meetings that people are unsure that they can prioritise Liam's values.
	Closed	Unaware	Disengaged

← More workable   Less workable →

Appendix 8F: Matrix completed with Liam

FIVE SENSES EXPERIENCING

AWAY FROM WHAT IS IMPORTANT ← → **TOWARDS WHAT IS IMPORTANT**

'IN YOUR HEAD' EXPERIENCING

3. What do you do that takes you away from what's important?

- Drinking and drugs to block thoughts out and give me energy.
- Spend ages dwelling on memories and losses, even though I know it doesn't help.
- Spend ages in my room, either out of it, sleeping or withdrawing from drink/drugs.
- If things get too overwhelming, blame myself.

4. What do I do to move towards what's important to me?

- Talk to the staff in the hostel.
- Make it to my appointments: support planning to book for housing, probation, substance use.
- Accept help.
- Make the effort to listen to music I love, dance, sing and connect with others without drugs or drink.
- Contact my children more often (but need help to get over predicting them rejecting me).

2. What internal stuff gets in the way when thinking about what's important?

- Memories and flashbacks of trauma.
- Predicting threat everywhere – constant high alert is exhausting. Also predict failure/rejection by children.
- Urge to score or drink.
- Thoughts of 'I am a failure'; 'I am an addict'; 'It's too late for me to change'; 'I'd be better off dead!'
- Sadness, disappointment, shame.
- Feeling of heaviness; no energy to do things.

1. What is important to you?

- A quiet life (some things need sorting for this to happen).
- Safety, stability and personal space: would like my own home.
- Connection with my children.
- Fun, humour, expressing myself dancing, singing, losing myself in music.

Guidance for completing the matrix and how it maps to being 'open', 'aware' and 'engaged'

- It can be completed in an assessment, in one session or built up over several sessions, or later in therapy to draw together all conversations so far.

- As the therapist, you can often model openness, awareness and engagement when using ACT. When introducing the matrix, you could do this by saying something like 'I want to invite you to talk through this sheet with me. I notice I'm having the thought that you might find it difficult (awareness, openness), but I really want to be helpful to you, so want to try it (engaged), if that is okay?'

- At each stage of completion, validate the client and slow the pace – even slower than the pace the client can manage. You might have conversations around each point they make; for example, you could ask about where values came from, when they have been most able to live in line with them (cultivating an 'engaged' stance). At any point you might ask them to stop and notice what thoughts they are noticing or what sensations they are feeling in their body as they talk (cultivating 'awareness'). If the opportunity arises, you could cultivate 'openness' by interweaving examples of defusion or acceptance (e.g. 'So you notice you have the thought that...' as an example of defusion, or 'Can you allow that feeling to be there?' as an example of acceptance).

- Start with the blank matrix – the axes, their labels and the headings in each quadrant.

- Explain: 'Every one of our behaviours can be thought about as either a move away from what's important to us, or a move towards what's important to us (engaged). We tend to get caught up in our heads – our thoughts, our stories about ourselves, difficult thoughts about the past or worries about the future. It can be good for our wellbeing to slow down and notice all five senses, in the moment' (aware).

- Start in the bottom right and invite the client to list their values (engaged).

- Draw the arrow from the bottom right to bottom left.

- Invite the client to share what 'internal stuff' (thoughts, feelings, sensations, urges, etc.) gets in the way when thinking about their values and list these in the bottom left. This highlights the inflexible flipside of 'openness' (by highlighting fusion with thoughts or feelings) and 'awareness' (highlighting past or future focus, self-stories/self-as-content, and 'in the head' rather than 'five senses' experiencing).

- Then move into the top left and ask what the person does when the internal stuff shows up, which takes them away from what is important to them (highlighting the psychologically inflexible flipside of 'openness': experiential avoidance).

- You can then draw an arrow from the top left to the bottom left and ask whether, when they do the things that they have just listed, whether any other internal stuff then comes up for them. Add these to the bottom left. These are usually along the lines of self-criticism, regret and shame about their attempts to cope (fusion, self-stories, past or future focus). Explore whether those additional thoughts and feelings lead to doing any other things that take them away from what is important (further experiential avoidance). If so, draw the arrow from the bottom to the top and add those to the top left quadrant. Reflect that they seem to be noticing a cycle of thoughts, feelings and behaviours that moves them away from what is important to them and leaves them stuck (thus cultivating awareness). You might at this point talk about whether this is workable/what it is costing them. You can invite them to try something different: to allow the internal stuff to be there (openness), focus on the present (awareness) and move towards what is important (engagement) anyway.

- Drawing the arrow from the top left to top right, you can then note any committed action they might take towards what is important to them (engagement). These general points will likely need developing into specific, measurable, attainable goals, but offer a starting point.

- Finally, reflect on how going through this process has meant they have stepped back and observed themselves, their thoughts and their behaviours, and that this is in itself a skill (awareness) that can help us make more informed choices to move towards what is important.

Subject Index

Author Index